W9-AWI-307

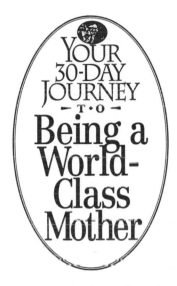

Your
30-DAY JOURNEY
— T · O —
Being a World-Class Mother

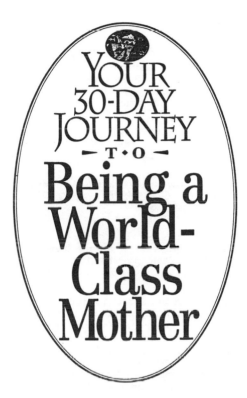

YOUR 30-DAY JOURNEY —T•O— Being a World-Class Mother

C. W. NEAL

A Division of Thomas Nelson Publishers
Nashville

Copyright © 1992 by Stephen Arterburn and Connie Neal

All rights reserved. Written permission must be secured from the publisher to use or reproduce any part of this book, except for brief quotations in critical reviews or articles.

Published in Nashville, Tennessee, by Oliver-Nelson Books, a division of Thomas Nelson, Inc., Publishers, and distributed in Canada by Lawson Falle, Ltd., Cambridge, Ontario.

Unless otherwise noted, the Bible version used in this publication is THE NEW KING JAMES VERSION. Copyright © 1979, 1980, 1982, Thomas Nelson, Inc., Publishers.

Scripture quotations noted NRSV are from the New Revised Standard Version of the Bible. Copyright © 1989 by the Division of Christian Education of the National Council of the Churches of Christ in the United States of America.

Every effort has been made to contact the owners or owners' agents of copyrighted material for permission to use their material. If copyrighted material has been included without the correct copyright notice or without permission, due to error or failure to locate owners/agents or otherwise, we apologize for the error or omission and ask that the owner or owner's agent contact Oliver-Nelson and supply appropriate information. Correct information will be included in any reprinting.

Library of Congress Cataloging-in-Publication Data

Neal, C. W. (Connie W.), 1958–
     Your 30-day journey to being a world-class mother / C.W. Neal.
         p.   cm.
     Includes bibliographical references (p.   ).
     ISBN 0-8407-9625-0 (pbk.)
     1. Motherhood. 2. Child rearing. I. Title. II. Title: Your thirty-day journey to being a world-class mother.
HQ759.N43   1992
649'.1—dc20   91–47907
                                                                              CIP

Printed in the United States of America.

1 2 3 4 5 6 — 97 96 95 94 93 92

To
my mother
Nina Perry
and
my stepmother
Edith Dodd Nixon
with love
and
appreciation

Contents

Introduction

THE DEMANDS OF modern-day mothering can leave us feeling inadequate when we compare ourselves with the images of remarkable women who seem able to do anything and everything, especially on a day when we can't find two socks that match!

THE JOURNEY

This book represents a journey you are invited to take. It has no power to change you until you begin to participate. Your willingness to dream and explore life, your love for your children, and your determination to try some new ways will bring about the changes you're hoping for.

TWO KINDS OF BOOKS

Two kinds of books deal with mothering and parenting: The kind that are helpful and encouraging and the kind that can make you feel quite impressed with the author but quite guilty and inadequate as a mother. The latter books become just so much clutter on your bookshelf and on your already burdened conscience.

My sincere hope is that this book will be transformed into a memento of something wonderful you chose to do for yourself and for your children; a memento of experiences that helped you become a better mother in tangible and memorable ways. Years from now, when you find it tucked away behind a line of books or perhaps under a bed, you may smile with a sense of your own accomplishment.

FRIENDLY COMPANIONS

I will be your companion and guide for the journey. And because education and support (that used to come from extended families) are missing for many women, I'll introduce you to other mothers who can offer helpful insights and act as role models.

Whether you are expecting your first child, have a house full of kids, or are adjusting to having your adult children out on their own, whether you see yourself as a candidate for mother of the year or as an unfit mother, you can gain confidence and feel satisfied with the relationships you have with each of your children. You can be a world-class mother.

When you come to the end of this journey, you will have achieved goals that are important to you, and you will reap the benefits that accompany the achievement of any worthy goal.

A View from Beyond

When we're in the midst of the day-to-day work of child rearing, it is common to lose sight of the true value of mothering. It's easy to let our view become narrow and to let little victories go by without recognition or applause. Every once in a while we need someone to remind us of what being a mother is really about. Only when you start from the perspective of viewing the whole picture can you take the right direction for your journey to be world-class mothers.

The plan for today is to relocate your perspective to a higher plane so that you can get a better view. In this way when you get to the point of setting goals, you will be able to focus on those of eternal value as well as those that deal with immediate demands.

Even those who are admired as being role models of a world-class mother know the feeling of getting lost in their tiny world while devoting themselves to the needs of their children. In *Simply Barbara Bush*, Barbara Bush describes the years she invested in caring for her five young children:

> This was a period, for me, of long days and short years; of diapers, runny noses, earaches, more Little

League games than you could believe possible, tonsils, and those unscheduled races to the hospital emergency room, Sunday School and church, of hours of urging homework, short chubby arms around your neck and sticky kisses; and experiencing bumpy moments—not many, but a few—of feeling that I'd never, ever be able to have fun again; and coping with the feeling that George Bush, in his excitement of starting a small company and traveling around the world, was having a lot of fun.

"I had moments where I was jealous of attractive young women, out in a man's world," she said later. "I would think, well, George is off on a trip doing all these exciting things and I'm sitting home with these absolutely brilliant children, who say one thing a week of interest."

These comments represent Barbara Bush's more narrow view of motherhood. The narrow view is absolutely true, and the feelings of being lost, bored, and overwhelmed are absolutely valid. It's a realistic view; it just isn't a view of the whole picture. If we see only the narrow view, we will grow discouraged. If we keep our eyes only on the path under our feet, we will not see enough sky to dream of flying.

These quotes represent real feelings and observations at particular times in her life. When she was asked to address the young women graduating from Wellesley College in June of 1990, Barbara Bush formulated her evaluation of the bigger picture of a woman's life into her speech.

As you set off from Wellesley, I hope that many of you will consider making three very special choices.

The first is to believe in something larger than yourself. . . . To get involved in some of the big ideas of your time. I chose literacy because I honestly believe that if more people could read, write and comprehend, we would be that much closer to solving so many of the problems plaguing our society.

Early on I made another choice which I hope you will make as well. Whether you are talking about education, career or service, you are talking about life . . . and life must have joy. It's supposed to be fun!

One of the reasons I made the most important decision of my life . . . to marry George Bush . . . is because he made me laugh. It's true, sometimes we've laughed through our tears . . . but that shared laughter has been one of our strongest bonds. Find the joy in life, because as Ferris Bueller said on his day off . . . "Life moves pretty fast. Ya don't stop and look around once in a while, ya gonna miss it!"

The third choice that must not be missed is to cherish your human connections: your relationships with friends and family. For several years, you've had impressed upon you the importance to your career of dedication and hard work. This is true, but as important as your obligations as a doctor, lawyer, or business leader will be, you are a human being first and those human connections—with spouses, with children, with friends—are the most important investments you will ever make.

At the end of your life, you will never regret not having passed one more test, not winning one more verdict or not closing one more deal. You will regret time not spent with a husband, a friend, a child or a parent. . . .

Whatever the era . . . whatever the times, one thing will never change: Fathers and mothers, if you have children . . . they must come first. You must read to your children, you must hug your children, you must love your children.

Your success as a family . . . our success as a society . . . depends *not* on what happens at the White House, but on what happens inside your house.

PERSONAL EVALUATION

- When is the last time that you recall reminding yourself, or having someone else point out, the greater value of what you do each day as a mother? What broadened your perspective?
- How do you feel about doing things to become more effective as a mother when you are focused only on the narrow view?

ACTION

Write a letter to yourself about how your success as a family and our success as a society is positively influenced by what you do each day as a mother.

REFLECTION

Take a few moments to consider Barbara Bush's advice about what is really important in life for every woman. If you are out of balance in one area or another, don't condemn yourself. Instead, give yourself permission to grow in these areas.

- In what way do you believe in and involve yourself in something larger than yourself? What "big ideas" are you committed to and how do you act upon that commitment?
- In what ways do you make decisions in the direction of joy? What do you do regularly that allows you to have fun and enjoy your life?
- How do you use your time and make your decisions to nurture the human connections in your life?

AFFIRMATION

The little things you do each day are important. They are the small battles that must be fought for your children's well-being. You also have something to offer in service to causes you believe in, causes larger than yourself. This involvement can be a good example for your children. You also deserve to have some joy in life. You deserve to have some fun!

Making a Commitment

Every journey involves a certain amount of work, the energy needed to get you from here to there. This journey is no different. To get where you want to be, you will need to expend your energies and abilities in the following ways: reading, thinking, looking at yourself, taking action, and reflecting on what you are learning and experiencing.

Each day's itinerary is set for you in general terms. You will make it apply to your particular situation. At every point along the way, you are free to choose your level of involvement. You don't have to use all the information provided or do everything suggested. Move as much as you can.

Completing the journey will take commitment on your part to continue on it, one day at a time, for the next 30 days. Each day's agenda will take at least thirty minutes, and you may find that you want to take more time than that, especially if you end up discussing the issues with a friend. Beyond the time required, you will need to commit yourself to find the courage and hope to keep going when the personal evaluation may feel uncomfortable.

Personal Evaluation

- Are you willing to make a 30-day commitment to your journey to being a world-class mother?

Action

My Personal Commitment

I, _____, am serious about my desire to be a world-class mother to *(list the names of your children here)* _____
_____.

I am willing to invest at least thirty minutes a day, from each of the next 30 days, to focus on this journey. I will plan to take this time *(circle one)* each morning, around noon, each afternoon, each evening, or before bedtime.

I understand that to reach this goal, I must be willing to grow on a personal level, to exercise the courage to look at myself honestly, and to endeavor to meet any challenges. I will do *my* best in all of these areas.

Since my goal is to be a world-class mother (not a "perfect mother") in the next 30 days, I will *not* focus my attention on how far I fall short of being the ideal mother. I will focus my attention on moving forward from where I am today toward what I want to be.

I make this commitment to myself this _____ day of _____, 19_____.

_____
Signature

REFLECTION

This section encourages you to reflect on what has happened and how you feel about it and to look for any insight that may help you on your personal journey. You can choose to do this by talking it over with a friend, writing your reflections in a private journal, praying about it, or just taking a few minutes to quiet yourself enough to think about your reactions to each day's journey. Take a moment now to decide which of these means of reflection you prefer. You may want to choose a combination. There is no right or wrong way. What's important is that you do what works best to help you gain insight about your journey.

Take a few moments today to reflect on the commitment you have made and how you're feeling about beginning this journey.

AFFIRMATION

You have already shown courage and a willingness to commit yourself. You're well on your way on the road to being a world-class mother!

FOOD FOR THOUGHT

One person with a commitment is worth one hundred who only have an interest.
—Mary Crowley

Finding a Companion for the Journey

Just as any trip can be more enjoyable when it's shared with someone, this journey could be enhanced by finding a companion to go with you. If you don't feel like this is a journey you would like to share with anyone, consider finding someone to use for support and feedback when you may feel you need help. Picture a long-distance runner who has support personnel driving alongside in a car. The runner goes through the paces on her own, but she has arranged to have a support team available whenever she shows signs of need. In this journey you will have moments when an encouraging voice, a proud smile, a nod of approval, or someone to talk things over with will prove extremely valuable.

PERSONAL EVALUATION

- Would you feel more comfortable "running" beside another person who is on a journey of her own, or would you like to have someone available to you while you're on your own journey?
- Take a moment to think of someone *whose*

company you enjoy to invite to come along. Or think of someone you would like to have available to encourage you and provide support while you go through the journey on your own. Identify the person you would most like to support you along the way. Also decide on a second choice if that person is unavailable.

- You may want to think of friends, mothers of your children's friends, relatives (ONLY if they are supportive and can keep your journey confidential), or members of your church or synagogue or other organizations.

ACTION

Contact the person you have in mind to be your companion for the journey.

REFLECTION

How do you feel about sharing this experience with someone else? Do you feel any sense of shame about admitting the need to become a better mother? Are you fortunate to have a circle of support persons so that finding someone was relatively easy? If you couldn't find someone today, are you willing to keep trying? For now, will you need to look to God to be your sole support until you can find a support person?

AFFIRMATION

Just reaching out for support and telling someone that you are beginning a journey like this take courage. You deserve to give yourself credit for your effort. If you didn't find anyone or were reluctant to ask, that's O.K., too.

FOOD FOR THOUGHT

Two are better than one, because they have a good reward for their toil. For if they fall, one will lift up the other; but woe to one who is alone and falls and does not have another to help.

—Ecclesiastes 4:9–10 NRSV

Two Perspectives on Mothering

Usually we will save the "doing" part of the journey until after you've read some information and had some things to think about. Today we will do things a little differently. We will use a puzzle to illustrate an important point and to be the basis for personal evaluation. I want to start by having you try to work the puzzle.

ACTION

Give yourself at least five minutes to try to work the puzzle on your own before you look ahead for the answer. This is not a trick. The puzzle can be completed while meeting all three required criteria.

Opposite are nine dots. Your task is to do the following: (1) connect all nine dots (2) with four straight lines (3) without lifting your pencil from the paper once you begin to draw. The puzzle is not solved until all three criteria have been met.

Let me give you a clue by telling you the mistakes most people make in their thinking that keep them from being able to solve the puzzle successfully. Then you can go back and look at the puzzle from a different perspective.

.   .   .

.   .   .

.   .   .

This puzzle can be solved successfully only if you *go beyond assumed limits*. Most people are frustrated while trying to solve the puzzle because they limit themselves. First, they tend initially to see the dots as a certain defined shape (a box). Research into the way the brain works has shown that when a human being already believes something, the mind rejects any options that would contradict the original belief. Second, once they have told themselves that they are looking at a box (since the brain will not readily accept unproven contradictory evidence), all they can see is the box. They automatically lock their minds into staying within the limits they have imposed. Third, they see what is before them; the dots and the conclusions they have drawn become real to them, but they do not see what is open to

13

them: the space surrounding the dots and the opportunities it represents.

Here is the correct way to solve the puzzle while
meeting all three criteria:

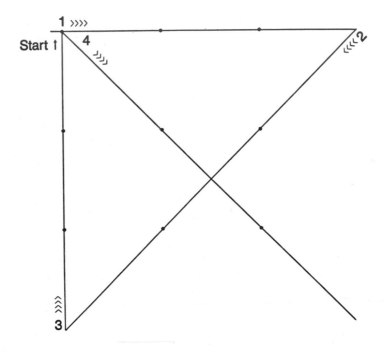

We limit our success in being world-class mothers
in the same way that most people limit their success
in working the puzzle.

First, we limit our vision. When we initially form

our opinion of what a "world-class mother" is, we may assume that being a world-class mother means doing all the tasks that we see "world-class mothers" doing—and doing them very well. So we limit our evaluation of how to be a world-class mother to those tasks "within the little box" we have defined mothering to be: patching skinned knees, resolving arguments, meeting emotional demands, doing laundry, preparing meals, cleaning the house, and so on.

But just like in trying to work the puzzle, doing those things better won't lead to satisfaction. Somehow all the dots of our lives (representing our mothering tasks, other responsibilities, relationships, and aspirations) don't seem to come together as neatly as they are supposed to do.

Second, we become so bogged down by the narrow view of what mothering entails, we may conclude that is all there is to it. We long for a greater sense of meaning.

Third, we don't see our significance in the lives of our children. We see the immediate but may miss the eternal. We see the days going by but may miss the possibilities and opportunities of a lifetime. We see each child: we know the name, birthday, shoe size, and social security number, but we may miss the incredible potential within each human spirit and may miss seeing the opportunity to bring out the best in each one.

Here is the conclusion I have drawn from the truth this puzzle illustrates: we can experience fulfillment in motherhood only when we go beyond the assumed limits of what it means to be a mother in terms of the tasks that we do, to see the eternal human value in ourselves and in each of our children. The narrator in the play *Our Town*, by Thornton Wilder, emphasizes this point when he says, "There's something way down deep that's eternal about every human being."

In *Our Town* the character Emily Gibbs dies in childbirth at age twenty-six. Against advice, Emily decides to go back to a happier time—her twelfth birthday. When she does, she sees her mother in a new light. Emily gains the eternal perspective that allows her to see the transcending value of a mother's life. She learns that whenever we lose sight of the eternal perspective, we lack understanding; whenever we are consumed with everyday business, we miss the deeper issues of life.

We don't understand much whenever we lose sight of the eternal perspective, whenever we are so consumed with the everyday business that we miss the life.

PERSONAL EVALUATION

Make two lists of what is important in mothering.

In the first list, write down things that are seen to be important if you look at mothering from a limited view with "inside the box" thinking.

In the second list, write down what you would consider to be important in mothering if you kept in mind the broader perspective, "beyond the box" thinking, that takes into account the possibilities of life and the eternal realities.

- Have you been judging yourself primarily on the evaluation of things in list #1 or list #2?
- Have you been frustrated by trying to be more effective with those things in list #1 without focusing on the fulfilling aspects of motherhood in list #2?

REFLECTION

Now, you're beginning to see yourself and your mothering in a new light. You are much more than what you do. Your value can be seen in who you are in your children's lives. When a close friend spoke of his mother, who died when he was eight, he didn't mention the things she did. Instead, he talked of the security he felt in her presence, the way he wanted to be good to make her proud of him.

You are what your children need. There is no adequate replacement for you in their lives, irrespective of how well you perform the tasks associated with mothering. This realization can give your self-image quite a boost if you let the truth of it settle into your heart. Perhaps you've experienced a scene similar to this one: A working mother is saying good-bye to her son at preschool, which has the best teachers and child care providers, all the latest toys and playground equipment, children's musical videos, great food, and an excellent program. As the mother gives the little boy a warm hug he looks up into her eyes and says, "But I want you, Mommy. I want you!" What a simple and beautiful endorsement of the value of being a mother.

I believe we need to be sold on ourselves as mothers. We need to sell ourselves on our influence in the lives of our children.

As you go through your routine tasks, ask yourself how you could make up a slogan that would show the greater value and true meaning in what you are doing, for example:

- It's not just making a peanut butter and jelly sandwich; it's building a strong body.
- It's not just wiping runny noses; it's preserving their health.
- It's not just giving them a ride to practice; it's an opportunity to hear what's on their hearts.
- It's not just saying their prayers; it's building a bridge to heaven.

Try to come up with at least ten slogans for the things you do each day.

AFFIRMATION

You are doing something positive right now to open your ears and your eyes so that you can understand more and be a world-class mother.

FOOD FOR THOUGHT

For the hearts of this people have grown dull. Their ears are hard of hearing, and their eyes they have closed, lest they should see with their eyes and hear with their ears, lest they should understand with their hearts and turn, so that I should heal them.

—Matthew 13:15

The Power of Being a Mother

Today you will get a sense of the power you have as a mother and find ways to use that power to bring out the best in your children.

When Abraham Lincoln was a young boy, his natural mother died. A year later his father married Mrs. Sarah Bush Johnson, a widow with two children of her own. The loving influence of this woman, who had taken on the role of mothering her lanky stepson and his sister, would change the course of world history.

Abraham Lincoln's greatness is evident. What, or whom, did he acknowledge as being most influential in bringing out the greatness in him? He is quoted as saying: "All that I am or hope to be, I owe to my angel mother." This is in reference to Sarah Bush Lincoln, the stepmother who believed in him, saw his potential, encouraged his pursuit of education (against the wishes of his father), and loved him dearly. He also said of her, "She has been my best friend in this world."

You are in a position to strongly influence how your children come to understand their inherent value. In this way you have power to shape the world, to create or destroy self-esteem, to inspire greatness and encourage accomplishment. One of the basic theories of sociology is that people will see themselves the way they believe the most important person in their lives sees them. When children are small, the mother is often the most important person in their lives. Therefore, what they perceive as your view of them will go a long way toward shaping the basis of how they see themselves.

Another illustration to show how a mother can influence her children to see themselves as valuable and worthwhile individuals is a personal one. When our family moved into our first home a few years ago, my mom bought a set of rose towels and sewed on lace trim that was mint and white. Although I thanked her for the housewarming gift, I never told her what that little extra touch of lace meant in my life. That special little touch told me that my mom believed I deserved a little extra. It said that Mom thought I deserved the beauty of lace. It also said that I was worth her time and the use of her special talents.

The power Sarah Bush Lincoln had in her son's life is not that different from the power my mom has in my life; it's the power of love, acceptance, and affirmation. Today you're going to look at how you accept, value, and affirm your children.

PERSONAL EVALUATION

"Mister Rogers' Neighborhood" is the longest-running children's program on public television. It has won virtually every award in its field. Why is Mr. Rogers so irresistible to children (and even some teens and adults who secretly watch his program)? The answer can probably be summed up in a few words: *respect, acceptance,* and *affirmation.*

If you want to turn to someone who will look you in the eye, validate your feelings, accept you as you are, and still affirm you, you can always depend on Mr. Rogers!

Sometimes as he goes out the door at the end of a TV "visit" he will say, "You've made this day a special day by just being you. There's only one person in the whole world like you. That's you yourself, and people can like you exactly like you are."

In the book *Mr. Rogers Talks to Parents,* he says,

It's so easy to say "Bad boy!" or "Bad girl!" to a child who spills or breaks or hits or bites or gets dirty. But the child is likely to hear "*I* am bad" rather than "What I *did* was bad," and a child who feels he or she is a bad person is also likely to feel unlovable. If we come to believe that we are unlovable, there's likely to be little motivation to avoid doing bad things.

It is possible for you to love your children dearly and for them to believe otherwise because you are not communicating that love in ways they clearly understand. If they falsely believe that you don't love them or like them, this has the same negative effect on self-image as if it were true.

You have the power and the opportunity to let your children experience the unconditional love and affirmation they long for. To exercise this power, you must first acknowledge that your children are worthwhile people and worthy of love even if they don't always behave as you want them to behave; then the love must be clearly communicated.

- Do you accept your children and love them unconditionally?
- Do your children believe that you love them, accept them, and appreciate them for who they are?
- Do you withhold love when you disapprove of their behavior?
- Are you trying to change them into the children you want instead of seeing them for who they are and accepting them as such?

ACTION

Plan today to do these three things with your children:

1. Pay close attention to something of interest to them. That means turning off the TV, putting down anything else you're looking at, and really listening with focused attention.

2. Maintain eye contact whenever they talk to you or you talk to them (except when you are driving). Note: This will make it extremely difficult to yell at them from the other room.

3. Display your affection through positive physical contact: hugs, pats on the back, high fives, a hand on the shoulder, and so on.

REFLECTION

Note what you did to communicate your love and any effects or responses you noticed.

FOOD FOR THOUGHT

They say that man is mighty,
He governs land and sea,
He wields a mighty scepter
O'er lesser powers that be;
But a mightier power and
   stronger
Man from his throne has hurled,
For the hand that rocks the cradle
Is the hand that rules the world.
   —William Ross Wallace

Breaking Free from Negative Influences

Some common beliefs may tend to stop you in your tracks when it comes to being a world-class mother. These beliefs stem from the primary understanding of child development that has been adopted and preached throughout our culture for many years. Today I want you to take a closer look at the bases for these beliefs and their negative effects on mothering.

False Belief #1

Your children's lives, their futures, and their happiness depend primarily on how well you train them.

This belief springs from the influence of what is known in psychological circles as behaviorism. Behaviorism teaches that each child is born as a clean slate for which every type of future is a real possibility if the child is properly trained. Behaviorists' concept of training was developed by experiments with laboratory animals whose behavior was modified by a series of rewards or punishments.

From these experiments on animals, they drew conclusions about human behavior and development. They disregarded the unique mix of genes that distinguish each person and the unique mix of humanity that determines, to a large extent, the range of possibilities for life. They disregarded the uniqueness of personality and temperament inherent in each human being from the beginning of life. Behavioral scientists also disregarded the truth that each person has a mind to choose and a free will.

Consider how these beliefs that have been accepted culturally may negatively affect your parenting. Behaviorism tells you that your children are "shaped" by your "training" of them. They are the result of the training or lack of training they have received. Therefore, if you don't train them properly, they will be warped forever, and you will be to blame!

False Belief #2

If you don't understand exactly what to do for each stage of children's lives or you fail them in some way, they will be irreparably damaged.

This belief has its roots in the teachings of Sigmund Freud, known as the father of psychoanalysis. Freudian psychology teaches that early experiences will largely determine how later life will be experienced.

According to Dr. Bruno Bettelheim in his book *A Good Enough Parent,* both leading doctrines of child psychology (behaviorism and Freudian theory) accepted in our modern culture emphasize that much depends on what the child experiences as he goes through the various stages involved in his growth toward maturity, and that a parent's handling of these situations is not only most important, but can be fatal when things go wrong. So now the modern parent is very well informed as to what he should worry about as he deals with the developing child! And, unfortunately, worry he does.

Given these doctrines, and given the fact that most people as youngsters have had no firsthand experience with raising children, it is little wonder that the conscientious parent becomes anxious about failing as a parent and fears that he may harm the child he loves.

False Belief #3

Successful mothering is very difficult.

Dr. Stella Chess and Dr. Alexander Thomas, renowned psychiatrists, have dedicated their lives and decades of research to the field of child development. They also happen to be husband and wife. In the closing message of their book *Know Your Child* they remark:

Louise Ames, of the Yale Gesell Institute of Development, a respected authority on child development, has said, "Given the fact that parenthood is probably the most difficult job in the world, I think it's a miracle that mothers do as well as they do. And most do very well indeed" (1983). Ames' purpose is to reassure mothers. Even if parenthood is very difficult, she tells us, most mothers can take comfort from her judgment that they "do very well."

But this last sentence of reassurance cannot cancel out her pronouncement that parenthood is a difficult job and that it is a miracle that mothers do it well. This viewpoint is entirely contrary to the thesis of this book, which we have tried to buttress with authoritative research evidence. Parenthood of a physically or mentally ill or handicapped child may be difficult, but not the parenthood of a normal child. It may be an important job, it may demand commitments of time and energy, but it is not difficult. Once the parents know that their child is flexible and adaptable, that they can experiment with different approaches without harming the baby, that they can easily learn to interpret their baby's signals and to communicate with their baby—all tasks which are not so difficult—then parenthood can become a relaxed and enjoyable experience.

False Belief #3 is the logical conclusion to False Beliefs #1 and #2. If children are blank slates whose entire development and future depend primarily on how well you train them, and if any mistakes you make will do them irreparable damage, it follows that successful mothering would be incredibly difficult.

The result of False Beliefs #1, #2, and #3 is primarily displayed in terms of fear and parental anxiety. Dr. Bruno Bettelheim discusses the fear resulting from these beliefs that can actually harm children. In essence, he believes parents may become so focused on how well they are doing as parents and their anxiety about not being good enough parents that they lose sight of the children and the children are left on their own.

You need to check to see if your focus of attention is self-centered or child-centered. If you are constantly analyzing yourself and allowing your motivation to be destroyed whenever you think you have failed to love up to some ideal standard, you will be absent emotionally when your children need you. Your anxieties about being a "good enough" mother can keep you from simply adoring your children and fulfilling their basic needs as best you can.

False Belief #4

You can't be a world-class mother because you are a bad person.

This sentiment grows from what has popularly become known as Toxic Shame. Shame, in the sense discussed here, is the belief that you are basically a flawed person. If others knew the real you, they would reject you. Therefore, the shame over inner brokenness or ugliness motivates you to pretend to be someone that others will accept. If you have this deep conviction that you are really an unworthy person, you will also conclude that you are an unworthy mother, incapable of meeting your children's needs.

This shameful conclusion may actually motivate

you to try to change the outside. However, you won't be able to conceive of effecting a deep transformation. In your mind, you are eternally flawed. The best you can do is to copy the outer behavior of other mothers, pretend to be the kind of mother you wish you were, and hope that is enough for your children. When we are ashamed of ourselves at the depth of our being, we will not be able to weather the normal failings every mother experiences. This discouragement will eventually cause us to shy away from examining ourselves, to fear asking for help and despair of trying to build deep relationships with our children. Instead we will gravitate toward those things that medicate the pain of living.

PERSONAL EVALUATION

Consider these false beliefs. Note to what degree you believe each statement and how it affects your mothering.

- Your child's life and happiness depend primarily on how well you train your child.
- If you don't understand exactly what to do for each stage of your child's life or fail in some way, your child will be irreparably damaged.
- Successful mothering is very difficult.
- You can't be a world-class mother because you are not good enough.

ACTION

If you tend to constantly be evaluating your performance, reserve self-examination for the time it takes you to work on your journey each day. Instead try to maintain a focus on your children.

If you suffer from deep feelings of shame that immobilize you, I suggest consulting a qualified therapist.

Focus on clearly defined goals that meet the needs of your children. Make commitments to these goals.

REFLECTION

Instead of these false beliefs, what are the truths that will give you the freedom to be the mother you long to be?

AFFIRMATION

New ideas give birth to transformation. Your willingness to stretch yourself by reexamining your beliefs will enable you to be a world-class mother. You have what it takes to raise your children and know the joy of a loving relationship with each of them.

FOOD FOR THOUGHT

And you shall know the truth, and the truth shall make you free.

—Jesus Christ

In Your Wildest Dreams

Today I dare you to dream. You don't have to tell anyone about your dreams or commit yourself to pursue any of them. For today I just want you to give yourself permission to dream. I dare you to dream of the admiration you desire from your children, the loving relationships with grown children and grandchildren, the happy holidays celebrated in your home.

I dare you to dream of bringing out the best in your children: seeing each talent fully developed and used to bring confidence into their lives; seeing each child as a productive, confident, educated adult, a person overflowing with love for others, serving the family and humanity; seeing them as people who face the evil in the world and in their own lives and fight against it; seeing them overcome evil with good; seeing them make wise choices, marry partners who treat them well, have joyous marriages, and raise their own children well.

I dare you to dream of exploring the world afresh with them, of reading the books you always wanted to read as a kid, of teaching them about life, love, and God; dream of expanding their knowledge of world history, geography, mathematics, language, sports, science, the arts, and literature; dream of the things they will learn, the discoveries they will make, and the lessons they will teach you!

I dare you to dream of achieving your best; of developing your talents, health, appearance, and abilities; of changing the world for the better and sharing the precious gift of yourself.

I dare you to dream of healing old wounds in your life; of breaking destructive family patterns that have tormented your ancestors; of escaping any cycles of bondage to addiction and compulsive behavior; of overcoming the debris of abuse in your life and the lives of your children; of being victorious in the face of those who doubt your abilities.

PERSONAL EVALUATION

- Are you accustomed to dreaming?
- Does dreaming seem dangerous to you?
- What keeps you from dreaming the best possible dreams for yourself and your family?

ACTION

Today your "action" will require an active imagination. Dare to let yourself imagine what life really would be like, in tangible and specific ways, if your dreams about mothering and your relationships with your children were the best they could be. To make your dreams more realistic, think in terms of your senses. What would the fulfillment of your dreams look like? What are the aromas, the feelings, the moods, the colors, and the sounds?

Fill in the following in your imagination. Don't just write down a description of what you think. Let yourself experience it in "vision" form.

In my wildest dreams about being a world-class mother:

- At the end, when I was looking back on my life, I would see . . .
- My children would grow up to be *(character qualities rather than occupation)* . . .
- My children would come to me and say . . .
- My children would overcome . . .
- My children would develop these attitudes to face life successfully . . .
- My children would regard themselves . . .
- My children would be spared . . .
- In eternity I would see them . . .

REFLECTION

How did it feel to allow yourself to dream?

FOOD FOR THOUGHT

Aim at heaven and you will get earth thrown in. Aim at earth and you get neither.

—C. S. Lewis, *Mere Christianity*

From a Dream to a Goal

To reach your dreams, you must return to reality (but with heaven in your heart). You must somehow get from the comfortable place of dreaming of what could be to the place where you are taking steps to actually lay hold of the dreams. Being known as a dreamer is altogether different from being known as a person who makes dreams come true.

To reach your dreams, you have to start taking steps in the right direction. If the previous days encouraged you to dabble in what it means to "live outside the little box," the following days will bring you back to the more narrow view "within the box" to deal realistically with your role and responsibilities as a mother.

PERSONAL EVALUATION

Here are the steps you will have to take to get from dreaming to making dreams come true:

- Seeing the dream so clearly that you become emotionally involved and motivated to take action to move in its direction.
- Identifying where you are now in relationship to

the desired "dream come true." If you have a clear view of the dream but are mistaken about how far you are from it, you will never reach your dream, no matter how much energy you expend.

- Setting objectives by writing down a specific description of the desired result.
- Listing the tasks that need to be done to reach the objective.
- Deciding who is responsible to make the tasks happen. You? You and someone else? Someone else who is accountable to you?
- Overcoming everything that stands in the way between you and your objective. Solving problems and filling needs are involved.
- Figuring out the timing. What is a reasonable amount of time to allow for the process? Set completion dates. Adjust your existing schedule and cooperate with the others involved.

Although you will take these steps, you will not experience them in the same way as other mothers. Therefore, the rest of the journey has to accommodate your individuality and the personal paths you will take to your dreams.

ACTION

- Are you ready to focus on the down-to-earth issues facing you as a mother?

- Are you ready to actively move in the direction of your dreams?

REFLECTION

Each day you will face the choice of taking part fully in the experience or doing it halfheartedly. The key to being able to commit yourself fully to each step along the way is to exercise *faith* that these steps will lead you to be a world-class mother.

If you have never before felt the confidence that you could become a world-class mother, I encourage you to take each step forward on this journey. Your dreams of better mothering can come true!

If you don't take constructive action to reach your dreams, you're left behind making excuses and explaining why you didn't really want what you had dreamed of anyway. Others escape to "dream land" in destructive ways. Human beings who give up on reaching their dreams often try to find ways to deaden the pain that comes in the absence of their dreams.

- Will you make the leap of faith that gives you the courage to deal with the down-to-earth issues?
- How do you feel as you are about to get down to the part of the journey where you stop thinking about mothering issues in general and start turning your attention inward?

AFFIRMATION

You can make it! You will know for yourself when you take each day and give it the best within you. You will soon be saying, "I can," because you will be able to look back and say, "I did."

FOOD FOR THOUGHT

A goal is a dream we are willing to take action on.
—Zig Ziglar

What's Your Motivation?

Motivation is the power that keeps you moving toward your goals. There are different kinds of motivating forces, from guilt to the need to please others, and each will get you moving initially. However, mothering is a lifelong commitment. To continue to strengthen mothering skills and affirm relationships, you will need the kind of motivation that endures and never fails.

Motivation That Doesn't Last—Guilt

Those motivated by guilt always have their "list." This mental list is where they keep track of every mistake they have made in raising their children, every emotional wound they may have inflicted, every activity they were unable to attend, every day they have worked outside the home, every cake they didn't bake, and so on.

Guilt motivation drives us in our attempt to "make it up to them." It's a form of motherly penance that keeps us running but never getting ahead. This growing burden of guilt will eventually crush the one trying to carry it.

Lunch Box Guilt

In the hilarious book *How to Be a Guilty Parent,* Glenn Collins shows how pervasive our parental guilt can be. Have you ever felt this kind of lunch box guilt?

MOMMIE: Ah, there's Fawn, our playmate here at the Little Purple Giraffe Day Care Center. What does little Fawnie have in her lunch box, hmmm?

FAWN: Kee.

MOMMIE: Kee? Ah, quiche, I see. Where'd you get that from, dear? Doggie bag from your dad's lunch? Oh, *Mom*, you say. Mom made it for you personally. Took her all yesterday afternoon, you say? Ah, but here's little Jennifer. What's she have in her Troy-Built lunch box, eh? What is that, dear?

JENNIFER: Buwwa bowwa.

MOMMIE: Huh? Let me see. Ah. *Bulgar Brownies*. Really? Mmm—so, well, nutritional. So marvelously healthy and, well, Bulgarian, don't you agree, Jennifer? Have a lovely snack. And what else is that, eh? You say *parvay*? A what? A pa-*vay*? Sweetie, shape your little bee-stung three-year-old lips so I can hear you better, honey. Try to talk a little more clearly, like my son, okay? So, how's your pavay? Oh, parfait, you're saying. Parfait! Oh, you say, a bee-cap parfait. And your dad just whipped it up in the Sanyo Food Processor this morning before he headed to the O.R., did he? (Aside to son:)

Marvin, boy. Shhh! Marvin. Listen to me, kid. That bunch of peanut butter sticks I pack for you every single morning? The peanut butter smeared on white bread, cut into strips, and dumped into wax paper? You tell them all that it's Nutted Wheat Wedges, right? Nutted Wheat Wedges? Your mom ground the nuts and your dad grew the wheat.

Marvin, got that? Marvin?

Outer Motivation

We are motivated outwardly when we try to impress someone else by keeping up the image that we are as good as someone else or by yielding to the pressure to please someone else without considering the unique needs of our children. The little voice tells us, "Your friend bakes cakes every week, so you should do some baking too." "Your neighbor home-schools her children, so you should home-school your children."

Those who are outwardly motivated usually have people in their lives that help keep them supplied with the sense that they aren't quite measuring up. Children will often try to use this type of pressure to get their way.

Mothers who work outside the home have to make decisions based on the reality of time constraints, not on arbitrary standards of comparison with other mothers. Sometimes we have to say no when our children want us to say yes. At these moments our children are apt to use a little outside pressure to motivate us to do things their way.

One working mother's daughter had a special event coming up at school that required a costume.

Her daughter tried various approaches to get her mother to make the costume instead of buying one. Finally she went to her mother and said, "Well, I guess you're not the *only* mother who's not making their child a costume."

"Oh, really?" she replied.

"Yeah. Brian's mom isn't going to make his costume either. Of course, Brian's mother is dead."

If this woman had been insecure in her priorities and had been outwardly motivated, she might have given in to her daughter's dramatic use of guilt. However, she was clear inwardly about what was important and why she had made her choice. She had clearly set her goals and her values. She was motivated by the positive motivation we will consider next.

Faith-Hope-Love Motivation

Faith-hope-love is the motivation that works for the long haul. It is not dependent on anyone else (except God, who is always available and willing to help). It comes from within, has tremendous power, is extremely positive, and can make any task or goal-seeking experience a wonderful adventure.

The faith element means that you are motivated by the belief that you can reach the goal, that you can be a world-class mother, that you can have fulfilling relationships with your children, that you can find ways to meet their needs within your means. Faith sees the reaching of the goal clearly and definitively, as though it were already a reality.

The hope element gets you through the tough spots. If faith sees the reaching, hope is the companion along the road, saying, "I know you can do this!" Hope encourages you to dare to dream and to keep moving in the right direction even when the going gets rough. Hope takes you closer to the goal that faith helps you see and believe in.

Love is the most powerful motivating force of all. It comes with remarkable credentials. According to the Bible, love is the one thing that *never fails*. It can bear all things and endure all things. When you empower your endeavors with the power of love (love for your children and loving respect for yourself), you will be able to do whatever it takes and go the distance to be a world-class mother.

PERSONAL EVALUATION

- In what ways do you see yourself driven by guilt motivation?
- In what ways do you see yourself driven by comparisons and outer motivation?
- In what ways do faith, hope, and love motivate you?

ACTION

Acknowledge your faith-hope-love motivation. This type of motivation will intensify as you investigate what mothering is all about. Your love for your children and your faith and hope will deepen.

REFLECTION

Allow yourself to feel the love you have for each child. Don't just think or talk about your love for them. Bask in the feelings that accompany the love you have for your children. Tonight after your children are asleep spend a few moments at each bedside. Don't hurry yourself. Reflect on that special little person who came forth from your life. Allow recollections to surface. Appreciate each one and the bond you share.

If your children are living away from home, close your eyes, think of them, and allow yourself to feel the love that stays within your heart.

AFFIRMATION

Your love for your children is the greatest power in the world.

FOOD FOR THOUGHT

Love suffers long and is kind; love does not envy; love does not parade itself, is not puffed up; does not behave rudely, does not seek its own, is not provoked, thinks no evil; does not rejoice in iniquity, but rejoices in the truth; bears all things, believes all things, hopes all things, endures all things. Love never fails. . . . And now abide faith, hope, and love, these three; but the greatest of these is love.

—Paul the Apostle

Rating a Mother's Role

Periodic evaluations provide a valuable function in our educational system. They measure the progress of the students in relationship to clearly defined categories of knowledge, skill, and performance. Measuring progress helps students see how well they are doing, where they need to improve, and where their strengths are. Periodic evaluations give students a growing sense of accomplishment as they master various skills and areas of knowledge over the course of time.

There is talk these days of redefining women's roles in society. How many women do you know who have defined their role as a mother in clear enough terms to allow them to measure their progress? Breaking your mothering role into clearly defined categories, rating how well you fulfill various aspects of your role, and conducting periodic evaluations will give you a growing sense of confidence and allow you to see where you need to focus your attention as you set goals.

Today you will make this kind of categorical evaluation for your own benefit. At the end of the journey you will rate yourself again to see where you have become more effective. One added benefit is that you will finally give yourself credit for the many things you do as a mother that are routinely taken for granted.

Perhaps you have never before done an evaluation. You may be like many women who rate themselves mentally all along, comparing themselves to other mothers. You probably haven't added up all that you do right in terms of fulfilling the needs of your children. This type of incomplete mental rating system can discourage you. You will find that by defining your role and measuring your progress you will be encouraged in your journey to being a world-class mother.

PERSONAL EVALUATION

- For each item listed, rate yourself on a scale of one to ten, ten being the top. If an item does not apply to your mothering role at this time (due to circumstances or the ages of the children), simply ignore that item.

Defining Role and Responsibilities

PROTECTION   *RATING*
1. Provide a safe environment ....
2. Teach safety rules ....
3. Personally supervise children ....
4. Provide trustworthy caregiver when away ....
5. Protect from other siblings (excessive teasing, physical aggression) ....

6. Teach self-protection skills ....
7. Provide preventive medical/dental care ....
8. Protect innocence/sexual boundaries. ....

PHYSICAL NEEDS   RATING
1. Furnish a healthy and balanced diet ....
2. Provide appropriate clothing ....
3. Provide medical care as needed ....
4. Provide dental care as needed ....
5. Provide appropriate level of privacy for sexual
   development and a healthy acceptance of gender .....
6. Provide and enforce necessary amounts of rest (sleep
   and quiet times while awake) ....

EDUCATION   RATING
1. Provide opportunity for education ....
2. Teach values at home ....
3. Answer questions and explain things ....
4. Provide a place for learning and study ....
5. Help them learn study skills ....
6. Supply tools for learning ....
7. Read to them and provide age-appropriate reading
   materials ....
8. Affirm their potential and progress ....
9. Provide extracurricular learning experiences ....
10. Recognize, encourage, and affirm strengths
    and talents ....

SOCIAL SKILLS   RATING
1. Provide social opportunities ....
2. Teach manners and social skills ....
3. Give correction in a nonshaming way, helping them feel
   confident in social settings ....
4. Allow and encourage participation in age-appropriate
   groups and organizations ....
5. Allow, monitor, and encourage age-appropriate
   friendships ....

PERSONAL HYGIENE

RATING

1. Provide a clean environment ....
2. Teach them at an appropriate age about personal cleanliness ....
3. Make sure hair is groomed ....
4. Check that clothing is clean, in good repair, and appropriate size, socially acceptable (not so out of style that they are ashamed) ....
5. Teach them how to keep living space reasonably clean and orderly ....

VALUES

RATING

1. Share personal values at their level ....
2. Provide value-related feedback to the media ....
3. Teach problem solving ....
4. Teach right from wrong ....
5. Set clearly defined limits and expectations for behavior
6. Give consistent discipline and correction ....
7. Maintain family traditions ....
8. Practice the values espoused ....
9. Admit mistakes and allow them to learn from Mother's life ....
10. Explain values in the context of religious beliefs ......

SPIRITUAL NOURISHMENT

RATING

1. Provide elements of beauty in life ....
2. Pray for and with them ....
3. Encourage hopes and dreams ....
4. Provide positive religious experiences ....
5. Read them Bible stories, stories that have moral lessons, etc. ....
6. Celebrate holy days in an uplifting and educational way
7. Allow and encourage them to wonder and to seek understanding of life ....
8. Allow them to voice doubts and to wrestle with beliefs in order to develop a personal faith ....
9. Affirm their rights as human beings to feel, think, perceive, interpret, want, choose, and imagine ....

ACTION

Circle any areas where you need to be more effective. You will use them later in the journey as the bases of your goals. Also record any comments you have about this exercise.

REFLECTION

For this exercise, getting feedback from someone who knows you and your relationship with your children would be helpful. Having an objective point of view may help you reflect on the accuracy of your perceptions.

Put this evaluation away for a while, and take some time later in the day to reflect on the experience and the feelings it aroused.

AFFIRMATION

The things you do well as a part of your mothering role have a positive effect on your children. Focus on those things. Keep up the good work!

FOOD FOR THOUGHT

And let us consider one another in order to stir up love and good works.

—Hebrews 10:24

Rating Mothering Relationships

Your role as a mother stays somewhat constant in terms of your responsibilities in raising and nurturing your children. In this regard, you can evaluate yourself in general terms for how well you fulfill those responsibilities to all your children. But when it comes to examining relationships, you must consider each relationship separately since each child is a unique individual.

Each relationship will be different because of many factors: the child's age and sex, your shared or differing interests, the season of your life when each was conceived, circumstances, health, the number and ages of the other children in the family. Accept this as an adventure, discovering each one's distinctiveness and the wonder of your relationship with each child.

PERSONAL EVALUATION

- For each item listed, rate yourself on a scale of one to ten. If an item doesn't apply to your child's age or to your unique situation, disregard it. If you have additional ideas for what you consider important parts of your relationships, add those and rate yourself there, too.

RATING MY RELATIONSHIP WITH _____
(child's name)

EMOTIONAL NOURISHMENT   RATING
1. Listen to the child . . . .
2. Validate feelings . . . .
3. Display physical affection . . . .
4. Maintain eye contact while talking . . . .
5. Verbally express love . . . .
6. Verbally express praise and appreciation of
   achievements . . . .
7. Offer encouragement . . . .
8. Give special attention . . . .
9. Attend special events . . . .

FUN TIMES   RATING
1. Play games together . . . .
2. Go enjoyable places together . . . .
3. Have unstructured time together . . . .
4. Do what the child enjoys . . . .
5. Listen to music and/or sing . . . .
6. Participate in sports or outdoor games . . . .
7. Enjoy toys . . . .
8. Read to or with the child . . . .
9. Create things together . . . .

THE CHILD AS AN INDIVIDUAL   RATING
1. Recognize talents and strengths . . . .
2. Recognize areas of weakness . . . .
3. Know close friends . . . .
4. Know school friends . . . .
5. Know fears and why . . . .
6. Know worries . . . .
7. Know favorite things (entertainers, food, books, color,
   subject of study, clothes, etc.) . . . .
8. Know hopes and dreams . . . .
9. Understand temperament . . . .
10. Know signs of when rest is needed . . . .

MY ATTITUDE TOWARD THE CHILD   *RATING*

1. Accept the child as he or she is . . . .
2. Affirm the right to feel as he or she does . . . .
3. Affirm the right to develop ideas . . . .
4. Affirm gender (I like that you are a boy or girl) . . . .
5. Affirm growing ability to care for self . . . .
6. Display and affirm unconditional love (apart from
   approval or disapproval of behavior) . . . .
7. Affirm healthy desires . . . .
8. Treat with respect . . . .
9. Practice the golden rule with the child . . . .
10. Support the child in ventures to learn and grow . . . .
11. Am fair and consistent . . . .
12. Show kindness . . . .

EXPECTATIONS   *RATING*

1. Confident that my expectations are in keeping with age
   level . . . .
2. Clearly express my expectations and listen to make
   sure child understands those expectations . . . .
3. Confident that my expectations are compatible with
   other healthy demands on the child's life (school, other
   parent's expectations, job, etc.) . . . .
4. Confident that my expectations are within the child's
   ability to perform . . . .

ACTION

Go back and circle any ratings where you need to be more effective in the relationship. Create a summary for each child of areas where you would like to strengthen the relationship. Then select one specific area to strengthen in your relationship with each child.

REFLECTION

Keep your reflections on this topic confidential. Each child must feel loved and appreciated fully. Children may misinterpret an evaluation of these relationships to mean that you love one more than another.

Take some time today to reflect on your relationship with each child and any theories you may have about why some relationships are stronger than others.

AFFIRMATION

By giving your attention to strengthening your relationships with your children, you are showing yourself and them respect.

Focusing on Each Child

Your mothering relationships will change as each child grows up. What is appropriate for one stage of life will be inappropriate for another stage. What is appropriate for the boys in the family may not be appropriate for the girls. What is appropriate for an introvert may not be appropriate for an extrovert. What is appropriate for one who breezes through schoolwork may be inappropriate for one who struggles academically. What works for a healthy child may not work for a child who suffers from a chronic illness. To be a world-class mother, you must consider the individuality of each child.

In *You and Your Child,* Charles Swindoll explains a popular Bible verse that parents have clung to as a promise for their children. The verse says, "Train up a child in the way he should go, and when he is old he will not depart from it." He brings out a distinction that is crucial for your journey:

At first glance, Prov. 22:6 would seem to deny the idea of individuality. But I want you to know it is just the opposite. Here's why.

Train up a child *in.* . . . The term *in* means "in keeping with," "in accordance to" the way he should go. In fact, in the New American Standard Bible you will notice verse 6 is margined with the literal rendering "according to his way." That is altogether different from *your* way. God is not saying, "Bring him up as you see him." Instead, He says, "If you want your training to be godly and wise, observe your child, be sensitive and alert so as to discover *his* way, and adapt your training accordingly. . . .

In every child God places in our arms, there is a bent, a set of characteristics already established. The bent is fixed and determined before he is given over to our care. The child is not, in fact, a pliable piece of clay. He has been set; he has been bent. And the parents who want to train this child correctly will discover that bent!

In taking some time to consider the special facets of each child's life, you will be able to identify the special bent and the special needs.

PERSONAL EVALUATION

Stella Chess and Alexander Thomas, professors of psychiatry at New York University Medical Center, have identified nine specific categories of temperament. Their book, *Know Your Child,* is designed to relieve the unfair burden of guilt heaped on mothers and to help parents recognize and bring out the best in each child. Developing a better understanding of each child's temperament can help you define the "bent" in his or her life. This can play a valuable role in helping you develop relationships sensitive to the individuality of each child.

Each category can be rated on a three-point scale: high, medium, or low. The following definitions are taken directly from the book. Read each one carefully, keeping each of your children in mind.

1. *Activity Level:* motor activity and the proportion of active and inactive periods. . . .
2. *Rhythmicity (Regularity):* the predictability or unpredictability of the timing of biological functions, such as hunger, sleep-wake cycle, and bowel elimination. . . .
3. *Approach or Withdrawal:* the nature of the initial response to a new situation or stimulus—a new food, person, or place. Approach responses are positive and may be displayed by mood expression (smiling, speech, facial expression) or motor activity (swallowing a new food, reaching for a new toy). Withdrawal reactions are negative and may be displayed by mood expression (crying, fussing, speech, facial expression) or motor activity (moving away, spitting new food out, pushing new toy away). . . .
4. *Adaptability:* long-term responses to new or altered situations. Here the concern is not the nature of the initial responses but the ease with which they are modified in desired directions. . . .
5. *Sensory Threshold:* the intensity level of stimulation necessary to evoke a discernible response, irrespective of the specific form the response may take (how sensitive are they to touch, taste, sound, sights, smells?). . . .
6. *Quality of Mood:* the amount of pleasant, joyful

and friendly behavior and mood expression, as contrasted with unpleasant crying and unfriendly behavior and mood expression. . . .

7. *Intensity of Reactions:* the energy level of response, positive or negative. . . .

8. *Distractibility:* the effectiveness of an outside stimulus in interfering without changing the direction of the child's ongoing behavior. . . .

9. *Persistence and Attention Span:* these two categories are usually related. Persistence refers to the continuation of an activity in the face of obstacles or difficulties. Attention span concerns the length of time a particular activity is pursued without interruption.

ACTION

Now that you have the format, consider each child and rate each area of temperament as high, medium, or low. Prepare a separate sheet for each category; then list each child's name and rating.

REFLECTION

Today reflect on what you know about your children. Consider some things that are facts (such as age), some things that are theory based on evidence you've collected (such as primary learning style; they learn more by doing than by listening), and some things that are intuitive (such as their emotional vulnerability at this stage in their lives).

- What did you realize about your children that you never thought of in those terms before?
- How can being sensitive to their particular temperaments allow you to be more understanding of them?
- How can you use your knowledge of their individual temperaments to affirm them and strengthen your relationships with them?

FOOD FOR THOUGHT

When we are out of sympathy with the young, then I think our work in this world is over.

—George MacDonald

Motivating Your Children

Motivating your children involves more than pasting shiny stars on a performance chart affixed to the refrigerator door. As a mother you are in a tremendous position to motivate your children every time you catch a glimmer of greatness. The best motivation in the world takes place when you recognize that which is special within your child and encourage its development. If you treat your children's talents with respect, point out what is special about these talents, and invest in helping your children develop their natural abilities, you will set in motion a positive motivational influence.

Although you are well acquainted with your children, there may be a tendency to miss the magic within them, given the hustle and bustle of everyday life. When you consider your children there are certain characteristics that are obvious to anyone—perhaps a quick wit, a way with words, a flair for artistic design, or an ability to move with the music. You may take these special qualities for granted. When you take the time to consider them more carefully, however, you discover added dimensions of potential you may have missed at first glance.

Jim Burns, an author of more than twenty books

on youth and youth work, tells of a $4 million governmental study conducted to discover what helps children learn. The $4 million answer: children learn better when they are personally motivated. Jim says he could have told them that for a mere $1 million!

You can best motivate your children by taking the time to recognize, acknowledge, and draw out what is already in them. They will learn how to do things, and they will learn that they are capable human beings who have tremendous abilities and talents as yet undiscovered, as yet untapped.

PERSONAL EVALUATION

Consider each child in the following ways:

Age and Developmental Stage

What special needs does a child this age have that it is my responsibility to take care of?

Sexuality

Does this child have a healthy, age-appropriate understanding of sexuality? Do I have open lines of communication with the child regarding sexual issues? Where is my child getting values and information regarding sexual issues? Has this child ever been sexually abused in any way? If so, has professional help been given to help the child recover from the abuse?

Personality and Relationship

Do I see him or her as an introvert or an extrovert? Do I accept the child, or do I try to change the personality to be something I prefer? Do our personalities seem to generally mesh easily?

Learning Style Type

Here is a brief description of learning styles:

1. *Innovative (feeling)*—learns from specific experiences; relates to people easily; likes to share ideas.
2. *Analytic (watching and listening)*—observes carefully before making a judgment; views things from different perspectives; seeks facts.
3. *Common Sense (thinking)*—logically analyzes ideas; plans systematically; acts upon intellectual understanding of situation.
4. *Dynamic (doing)*—gets things done; takes risks; prefers trial-and-error method.

Which of the four learning styles best describes what I have observed about this child?

Physical Health

General health is excellent, good, fair, or poor. Does a physical limitation or health problem limit the ability to enjoy life as other children?

Talents and Special Abilities

What are the areas of apparent talent: music, art, mechanical abilities, drama, computers, poetry, creative writing, debate, athletics? What special skills and abilities has the child developed by following interests?

Education and Intellectual Abilities

The intelligence level is genius, above average, average, below average, developmentally disabled in some way. What subjects does the child enjoy learning about? What subjects are not enjoyed? What are favorite books? What does he or she consider to be the greatest accomplishment?

Interests and Hobbies

How is free time spent? What are the child's hobbies, favorite musical group or musical artist, favorite TV shows, and favorite sports? What does the child want to be when he or she grows up?

Social Skills

Does the child know how to interact well with others of the same age? Does the child know how to resolve differences? Does the child understand and practice socially acceptable behavior and manners?

Interaction within the Family

How does the child get along with siblings? Can I identify the child as playing one of the roles identified generally in dysfunctional families? If so, which one (the caretaker, scapegoat/distracter, super-achiever/hero, quiet/lost child, mascot/comedian)?

Are there open lines of communication: with father? with mother?

Spiritual Development

How extensive are the child's spiritual interests? Does the child have a personal faith in God? Does the child want to attend religious functions?

Areas of Brokenness

Has the child experienced physical, sexual, or other forms of abuse? Has the child experienced any kind of physical, medical, or accidental trauma that had an apparent emotional effect? Has the child lived in a home where one or more family members were under the influence of addictions and/or compulsions? Has the child lived through seasons when basic needs were neglected? Has the child been separated from one or both parents for any length of time? Has the child gone through the separation or divorce of parents? Has the child lost someone through death or a move? Has the child been allowed or assisted to grieve these losses?

ACTION

Now that you've considered each child in these ways, identify any areas you want to learn more about. What are they? Write three good attributes or interests you see in each child. Take specific action to affirm and bring out the good in each child.

Make a list of anything you want to do for each

child to motivate further healthy development of his or her special qualities. For example, if your child shows good coordination and love of music, the specific action you might choose could be to provide dance lessons or the opportunity to join a marching band's drill team.

REFLECTION

This evaluation takes a great deal of concentration and emotional energy. Don't spend too much time reflecting on this right now if you don't feel like it. If you do feel like reflecting on today's journey, you might find it helpful to talk over your observations with someone. You could even use the exercise as a chance to open up interesting discussions with your older children.

AFFIRMATION

God created you with the ability to be a world-class mother. He has put within you the resources you need to raise your children. One of your greatest natural resources as a mother is the ability to recognize and appreciate the potential in each of your children.

FOOD FOR THOUGHT

Train children in the right way, and when old, they will not stray.

—Proverbs 22:6 NRSV

Assessing Damage and Beginning Recovery

We live in a broken world where people sometimes abuse and hurt one another. In their relative powerlessness, children are vulnerable to abuse. News reports and talk shows have made childhood abuse a topic familiar to all of us.

Today's stop is not a pleasant one. However, it is your responsibility to protect your children from abuse. Every mother needs to be able to identify the signs of abuse and know how to get help when abuse is suspected.

Be alert to possible warning signs, and be willing to see and hear the truth of what has happened. Some common warning signs of abuse include the following:

- Experiencing sleep disturbances
- Reporting to you that inappropriate behavior has happened
- Showing physical signs of irritation of sexual organs or sexually transmitted disease
- Having physical marks or bruises that cannot be identified as having happened by accident

- Acting out sexually explicit scenes or being sexually precocious in play with peers and/or dolls
- Engaging in excessive masturbation
- Engaging in delinquent acts such as running away or being overtly seductive or promiscuous
- Displaying learning problems and inability to concentrate
- Experiencing poor peer relationships
- Escaping into fantasy
- Reverting to infantile behavior
- Being withdrawn, suicidal, hopeless, and/or helpless
- Exhibiting self-destructive behavior, such as drug abuse or alcohol abuse
- Showing a lack of trust and disdain for adults and authority figures
- Exhibiting extremely low self-esteem

The presence of these signs does not mean that a child has been abused. They do mean that something is not as it should be. Whenever that is the case, become a detective to determine the real cause of the "symptoms."

In the case of some severe trauma, the child may repress the experience and not have a conscious memory of it. When this happens, the pain of the abuse may not be expressed emotionally and may be felt through physical symptoms of pain. The first line of investigation for physical symptoms is consulting a medical doctor. If there is no apparent reason for severe or chronic pain, you may need to talk to health care professionals who are expert at diagnosing emotional injuries that can lead to physical symptoms.

If you suspect that abuse may have occurred to your child, call your local agency for child protective services. Trained professionals there know how to determine whether abuse has occurred, and they can help your family deal with whatever has occurred. They can also refer you to people, organizations, and resources to bring healing to an abused child.

There is an organization called Parents Anonymous that offers free, *anonymous* consultation, professional help, and support related to parenting issues, including child abuse. You can call them without ever letting them know who you are. You can talk openly about your concerns, your fears, your problems. The toll-free number is 800-421-0353.

PERSONAL EVALUATION

- Have you ever noticed the warning signs of abuse in your children?
- Are you willing to take the steps needed to cope with abuse?
- Were you ever abused as a child?

ACTION

If you have any suspicion that your child may have experienced abuse, make it one of your highest goals to get help for the child. Put this objective above any other you may have chosen to work on in the area of your role and responsibilities. Immediately talk over your concerns with someone who understands and can point you in the direction of help.

REFLECTION

Families who have experienced the devastation of abuse feel quite alone. It's not an easy topic to talk about. However, if your family has been touched by abuse, you are not alone. Statistics show that one of four girls and one of eight boys are abused sexually by the age of eighteen. Unfortunately, no segment of the population is risk free. The incidence of abuse is basically the same for churched and nonchurched families. The point is, you are not alone! Reach out for help.

There are help and hope for healing and recovery once the abuse is stopped.

FOOD FOR THOUGHT

The LORD builds up Jerusalem;
    he gathers the outcasts of Israel.
He heals the brokenhearted,
    and binds up their wounds.
        —Psalm 147:2–3 NRSV

Defining Goals

Today you will clearly define your goals. All you have to do is to look back over the exercises you have already completed and choose what you are willing to take action on at this point in your life. You will obviously not be able to achieve all the many things you have identified as being of interest to you. Select a few goals to focus on initially. Then as you successfully achieve them, you can replace them with new goals.

My idea of a world-class mother is depicted in the three spheres of this diagram:

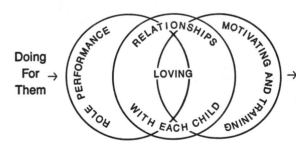

A world-class mother has a positive balance in these three areas of mothering: the doing, the loving, and the launching. So, you will be setting goals in three primary areas: (1) revitalizing your performance of your mothering role, (2) strengthening your relationship with each child, and (3) motivating your children to bring out the best in them.

PERSONAL EVALUATION

Step One

Go back to "Day 10: Rating a Mother's Role." Pick one of the areas in which you wanted to be more effective.

Step Two

Go back to "Day 11: Rating Mothering Relationships." Pick one area in which you wanted to strengthen your relationship with each child. You may have the same area of interest for all of your children.

Step Three

Look back over the information you have written about the unique qualities of each of your children. Pick one area for each child where you would like to take action to help bring out the best in him or her.

Continually reaching goals in these three areas will lead to being a world-class mother. How will you know when you have reached your goals? You will evaluate your progress on Day 29 of the journey.

Now you need to come up with specific actions to take within the next two weeks. The short-term objectives will take you in the direction of your goals.

Step Four

Write out a clear and specific description of each goal so that you will be able to tell in two weeks if you have kept your commitment to pursue it. You may want to define the immediate and long-term versions of the same goal.

Let's use a relationship-strengthening goal as an example. *In my relationship with Marnie (age fifteen) I will make a point of spending more time with her when we can talk without the distraction of the other children. I will create opportunities when she can talk freely (inviting her to go with me anywhere that I am planning to go on my own, taking a snack to her in her room in the evening, driving her whenever she needs a ride somewhere). I will listen to her concerns, her ideas, and her feelings. I will make a point of trying to understand her perspective. I will know that I have reached this goal when I consistently am able to reflect back to her what she has related to me and have her confirm that I am understanding her fully.*

ACTION

Create a mothering notebook. Use a three-ring binder, and divide it into three sections: "Being More

Effective in My Performance of Mothering Roles and Responsibilities"; "Strengthening My Relationships with My Children"; and "Motivating: Affirming and Bringing Out the Best in My Children." For each section make up a form with these headings— "Dream," "Goals," "Tasks," "People Involved," "Timing," "Checkup"—and photocopy several of them. Initially you will need the number of children you have plus two more.

Now that your thinking is clarified in terms of a few specific goals, you will take the information from your evaluations and slot it into these forms.

- In the "Dream" column, write down the long-term result that your objective will lead you toward.
- In the "Goals" column, write down the specific measurable result you are trying to achieve. Ask yourself, How will I know when I achieve this goal?
- In the "Tasks" column, write down all the tasks involved.
- In the "People Involved" column, write down who is responsible for each task or who you need to cooperate with to complete the task.
- In the "Timing" column, write down the date you plan to complete each task and the overall goal, take note of who else has to accommodate a schedule for you to be able to complete each task and reach your goal in the time required.
- In the "Checkup" column, write the date you are

checking to see how you are doing and how near you are to completing the task and reaching the goal.

REFLECTION

- How are you reacting to the switch to doing the actual work of setting specific goals?

AFFIRMATION

You have done a good deal of work in applying your abilities to identify and set specific goals. Your efforts will pay off.

FOOD FOR THOUGHT

And let us not grow weary while doing good, for in due season we shall reap if we do not lose heart.
> —Paul the Apostle

Coping with Time Limitations

You probably don't have much spare time these days. But you'll need extra time in your calendar so that you can add these new commitments. One way to start is to chronicle your days for the next two weeks.

Step One

Sketch out a diagram that depicts twenty-four hours for each day in the coming two weeks (if you already keep a calendar, you will need to refer to the plans you have recorded for the next two weeks).

Step Two

Fill in the hours that you regularly spend sleeping, eating, grooming, and taking care of other physical necessities.

Step Three

Fill in the hours that are already committed to on-going activities that you are not in a position to change, such as school, work, church, and so on.

Step Four

Fill in all the appointments you have planned for

the next two weeks, such as going to the dentist or attending meetings, sporting events, social events, and so on.

Anything left open on your calendar should represent areas of opportunity: opportunities to fulfill your responsibilities, to take care of yourself, and to move in the direction of achieving your goals.

Step Five

Make a list of the things that you need to do and/or want to do in the coming two weeks. (Be sure to include your new goals in this category.)

Step Six

Read over the list, and rank each item with a V = very important to me, M = moderately important to me, or O = optional (not really important to me). Reconsider what is truly important in light of your current focus on being a world-class mother.

Step Seven

Turn your short-term goals into commitments by taking them from the list of random items on your floating "to do" list and scheduling them into your daily calendar as appointments. If they do not fit into appointed times, commit them to a specific day, such as Thursday afternoon or evening.

This commitment should be realistic or you will become discouraged. If your schedule is too tight, you can adjust the application of your goals into somewhat shorter time segments or arrange to set aside other activities that are less important.

FOOD FOR THOUGHT

Dost thou love life? Then do not squander time, for that's the stuff life is made of.

—Benjamin Franklin

Coping with Financial Limitations

You may often feel that to meet your children's needs, you really could use more money. The fact of the matter is that having money does offer more freedom of choice in terms of how to meet their needs. Financial security also offers relief from the pressures that can seem overwhelming when you're doing your best to make ends meet (and they still don't). The stress of struggling financially while also trying to focus your attention on the needs of your children can be terribly upsetting. It may seem that financial limitations are a major limitation to mothering.

Financial difficulties can have a debilitating effect on us as parents, especially in single-parent and dual-income families where the lack of financial reserves translates into having to spend more time than you would like away from your children. I don't want to make light of the weight that financial stress can place on family relationships. However, I want to encourage you to consider whether you are drawing incorrect conclusions about how your financial status affects your ability to be the kind of mother you want to be.

What your children really need from you is not limited by the amount of money you have. What your children really need is for you to convey to them a positive self-image about themselves.

One young mother of limited means has three children. She finds creative ways to meet their needs for clothing and nutritious meals and material possessions. And she and her husband give their kids love and plenty of one-on-one attention. When asked the secret of how she seemed to be able to keep her kids happy on such a tight budget, she responded, "Some people haven't learned the fine art of lying on the floor and letting their children crawl all over them." She realized that what they need the most is their mom.

PERSONAL EVALUATION

- How does your financial status affect your view of your ability to meet your children's needs?
- What image of the family do you reflect to your children? Poor? Well-off? Comfortable?

ACTION

Review the family budget in light of the values you worked out on Day 4. Determine what financial commitments need to be made, changed, or abolished in order to put your financial influence to work to achieve what is truly important in the lives of the children. Lie on the floor and let your children crawl on you. Spend time with them whenever you can, and give them your undivided attention.

FOOD FOR THOUGHT

You may have tangible wealth untold;
Caskets of jewels and coffers of gold.
Richer than I you can never be—
I had a mother who read to me.
　　　　　　　　—Strickland Gillian

Identifying Where You Need Help

No one can achieve goals alone, especially when those goals concern human relationships. The purpose of today's stop is to accurately assess where you will need help and what kind of help you will need.

Guard against two extremes. A strongly independent person tends to resist admitting she needs help or asking for help. She wants to do it herself! This person will tend to take longer and work harder before she is willing to ask for help, and then she will seek help only if she has exhausted her own resources. At the other extreme is the dependent person who sees herself as helpless. This person is inclined to find someone else to help her or to do for her what she could do for herself if she would apply herself to the task. To reach your goals successfully, you have to strike a balance between determined independence and clinging dependence.

PERSONAL EVALUATION

- Are you the type of person who tends to be strongly independent (superresponsible) and resists admitting when you really need help?

- Are you the type of person who tends to be overly dependent (irresponsible or codependent) and asks for help when you really could do more for yourself if you tried?
- Can you identify anything in your life that may have influenced this type of response?
- When have you had a positive experience by receiving help?

ACTION

Review the goals you've written in your notebook. To achieve those goals, you will need knowledge, practical help, and support. Your job today is to identify every area where you are not completely self-sufficient to reach your goals. Add a section to your notebook titled "Help." Transfer over the goals you have already chosen, and write down:

- What do you feel that you will need help to know, to understand, to do, to continue doing?
- In what areas will you need support?
- Whose cooperation will you seek?

After you have completed a list of the help you need to reach your specified goals for this journey, flip back through the pages of this book and list other areas of interest where you will need help to continue growing as a mother and as a person.

REFLECTION

You may feel awkward about admitting your need for help. Don't allow that awkwardness to hold you back from reaching significant goals. Everyone needs help.

AFFIRMATION

It takes a lot of courage to look at yourself honestly and acknowledge areas where you need help. By acknowledging where you need help, you are moving toward being a world-class mother.

FOOD FOR THOUGHT

You do not have because you do not ask.
—James 4:2

Overcoming Whatever Stands in Your Way

Everyone will face problems and experience needs in the journey toward goals. How you perceive and deal with problems and needs determines whether or not you will reach your dreams. To overcome the obstacles between you and the achievement of your goals, you have to learn to have a positive attitude. If you see a problem as a challenge, you will tackle it, turn it into an opportunity, and make it work for you. Those who learn to solve problems and fill needs will become achievers. Those who take refuge behind their problems and needs will never achieve their goals.

Every disappointment, difficulty, problem, or need can be seen as a stumbling block or a stepping-stone. When you learn to welcome every obstacle as an opportunity to overcome, you will be able to reach any worthy goal. You will enjoy a sense of adventure instead of discouragement.

With God's help you could turn around the disappointments and deprivation you have experienced and find a way to win by seeing life in a new light.

PERSONAL EVALUATION

- What are the obstacles that keep you from being the world-class mother you want to be?

- Do these obstacles stop you or challenge you?
- How have you overcome obstacles in the past to achieve your goals?

ACTION

Draw a line down the middle of a sheet of paper and list on one side all the problems, obstacles and unfulfilled needs standing in your way. Take a positive attitude toward each one and turn them into opportunities. List the opportunities on the other side. For example:

Obstacle	Opportunity
• I have limited finances.	I have the opportunity to make my life more productive by learning to manage money.
• I am tired.	I have the opportunity to find help and rearrange my schedule so I can get rest.
• I can't get my children to obey me.	I have the opportunity to learn how to discipline and teach my children to be well behaved.

REFLECTION

When you see only the obstacle without considering the opportunity, what is the effect on your attitude?

When you hear yourself making positive statements, what is the effect on your attitude and motivation to continue seeking your goals?

AFFIRMATION

You have plenty of opportunities for personal growth and the exercise that develop a positive attitude. You can choose to dwell on the positive. The power of positive choices is available to you. You can learn to see obstacles as opportunities.

FOOD FOR THOUGHT

Experience is not what happens to you; it is what you do with what happens to you.

—Aldous Huxley

Considering Your Mother

You can learn much from your mother if you seek to find the good in her life and example. Finding good in your mother's life and learning from it are choices you make. These choices don't hinge on how well your mother performed her role or how good a relationship you have with her. Consider and acknowledge what your mother did right. See the love, even if it wasn't always communicated perfectly.

A human being may fail in countless ways. When that human being is your mother and the failing is in the area of meeting your needs, you tend to feel the pain of that failure to the core of your being. Perhaps your mother didn't give you the care and attention that you needed. Perhaps she hurt you terribly or rejected you or constantly criticized you. Perhaps she died when you were young or was incapacitated in some way. Perhaps your mother was consumed by some addiction or compulsion that removed her from you emotionally. Perhaps your mother abused you or allowed someone else to abuse you without coming to your rescue.

The bookstore windows have been awash in recent years with a wide variety of "I blame my mother" books. I find myself wondering if the authors of these books will ever get beyond the identity of being children who were not taken care of by their mothers to develop into whole, balanced people. I see the place for an honest struggle with the pain of such a deep disappointment. I understand the need to face and process the disturbed emotions stirred up when a child has been neglected or otherwise abused. However, I also see the danger of getting stuck in the briar patch of bitterness.

In the Bible the visual picture of forgiveness is that of a list of offenses nailed to a cross with the blood of Jesus "having wiped out the handwriting of requirements that was against us" (Col. 2:14). That referred to the customary legal practice of listing on parchment the offenses for which the condemned person had been convicted. The list explained to anyone passing by why the person deserved to be punished. When the blood of the person ran down over the list as he was dying, the death was accepted as having wiped out the handwriting of requirements held against him. Saying that Jesus gave forgiveness by having nailed our offenses to the cross shows that the prerequisite to forgiveness is that there is a list of offenses for which we have been convicted.

This image of being convicted before you can truly be forgiven and pardoned also applies to the process of forgiving others. You cannot truly forgive others until you have truly convicted them of all the requirements you have against them. When you list all the ways that your mother hurt you, all the pain that you experienced because (for whatever reasons) she failed to fulfill her responsibilities as your mother, then you can take the list you have against her and leave it at the foot of the cross. You cannot give her God's forgiveness. That is her choice as to whether she will receive it. But you can acknowledge that what she did or failed to do on your behalf was wrong and damaging (if it was), and that you are choosing to let go of your demands that she pay you back for the damage done. In this way you can acknowledge the value of your feelings: you can honestly deal with the debris in your life that has resulted from her failings; and you can proceed on your journey toward wholeness without getting bogged down with bitterness.

To truly forgive, you must not excuse the actual violations of what is right. To truly forgive, you must first convict the guilty party of every offense, then nail those offenses to the foot of the cross. Perhaps you still feel strongly that she needs to be held accountable for the damage she caused. You just forgive and still hold her accountable, honestly acknowledging her responsibilities and the consequences of her failings. You can choose to transfer that weight off your shoulders onto God or other governing authorities (in some cases where laws have been violated). Be assured that God promises to take care of the matter in His own way and time. Forgiveness is letting go of your personal resentments and bitterness. It will take time, but you can begin by determining to con-

tinue in the process until you experience the freedom that forgiveness gives you from her control of
your life.

PERSONAL EVALUATION

- Have you tried to forgive your mother for the
  hurts you experienced in your relationship?
- Have you ever allowed yourself to specify the "offenses" you hold against her in your heart as a
  prerequisite for forgiveness?
- Have you been able to take responsibility for
  your life regardless of how well or poorly your
  mother took care of you?

ACTION

Make a list of everything you are grateful for in reference to your mother. Take an honest look at any
resentment or deep sadness lurking in your heart in
the estimation of your mother. You are not looking
for anything that is not there already. You may have
been fortunate to have maintained a positive relationship with your mother so that hurts were re-
solved when they occurred. If that is the case,
certainly don't make up any resentments. However,
if you have ignored or tried to brush aside valid offenses against you by your mother, today is the day to
convict her in your own mind of those offenses. Once
you have found her guilty of the "sins" you see in her,

you are to acknowledge the validity of the pain they caused in your life, admit they deserve to be punished, but declare your choice to pardon her.

Pretend that you are the one making out the same kind of legal statement of offenses referred to as being nailed to the cross. Describe how they affected you. Once you have emptied out all that you are holding against her, you can take that list before God and pray something like this:

Dear God,

Here is the list of offenses that I feel my mother has committed against me. Thank You that You respect our lives enough to recognize the need for accountability for how we hurt those we love. I don't want to hold on to these anymore. I will give them over to You and trust that You and she can work out any further arrangements. Amen!

REFLECTION

The Bible says that love covers a multitude of sins (James 5:20). Consider how the love in your heart can help to heal any old hurts. Consider how your mother's love positively affects your life.

The issue of forgiveness is worthy of careful consideration. No one is perfect. Everyone needs forgiveness from God and from others. Remember, the measurement that you use to judge your mother will be the very same measurement that will be used to measure your life. Don't let your identity become lost in hatred and bitterness toward your mother for her failings. Work through forgiveness, and grieve your losses for the sake of yourself and your children.

FOOD FOR THOUGHT

You don't have to excuse; you do need to forgive.

Caring for Yourself

To be a world-class mother, you need to experience the balanced life of a whole person, not just focus on one aspect of your life related to your children. You need to take care of yourself so that you will be healthy enough to meet your children's needs and be a good role model.

In *The American Woman*, Alice S. Rossi was quoted as saying, "If a woman's adult efforts are concentrated exclusively on her children, she is more likely to stifle than broaden her children's perspective and preparation for adult life."

The care you give to your health and appearance is a gift to your children. As children begin to interact socially, they become aware of how well they and their family fit into the culture. A mother who is well-groomed, neat, and clean demonstrates self-respect and helps her children build positive self-images by association. During grade school years children's peers pay close attention to appearances. How you regard and care for yourself will be a marker for your children as they form opinions of what kind of persons they are. You are also the model your children see as they learn to care for themselves. When you care for yourself, you are demonstrating care for your children.

You need to make sure that you have met your basic health needs. This includes physical, emotional, spiritual, and mental health. Some women lose themselves in tending for the needs of their children and others while neglecting their own basic needs. Our culture has made a caricatured heroine of the mother who claims to have no needs or wants other than to supply the needs of those she loves. In reality, however, if you do not take responsibility for making sure your basic needs are met, you will not be able to maintain giving to the needs of your loved ones in healthy ways. You may continue to give, but over the course of time your reserves will run dry and resentment may take hold of your heart. It's best to keep yourself whole and healthy so that you can live a balanced life of self-care and care for others.

Sometimes self-care means that you have to look at the areas of pain in your life. The purpose in considering the unresolved grief and pain of your childhood is not to drag up the past. However, for many people the pain of the past intrudes into family relationships of the present.

Face the pain of the past that you have not been able to escape or to fully resolve. The problems of the present may all be tied to the brokenness experienced in your earlier life. The problems may include substance abuse, alcoholism, sexual addictions and compulsions, addiction to chaos, self-sabotage, child abuse, compulsive overeating, overspending, over-working, overchurching (and almost any other over-anything else). In these cases your ability to express the love you have for your child may be severely impaired if you do not resolve your own problems.

PERSONAL EVALUATION

Physically. Are you getting enough good food, rest, exercise, and medical care? Are your grooming habits showing positive respect for your body? Do you buy yourself the things you need to care for your appearance and ongoing health care (clothing, vitamins, cosmetics, hair accessories, and so on)?

Emotionally. Are you sensitive to your own emotional needs for nurturing? Do you allow yourself to share your feelings with someone who is supportive and understanding? Do you give yourself some slack when you may be overcome with uncomfortable emotions such as anger, disappointment, and fear, or do you reject those feelings and condemn yourself whenever they arise? Do you treat yourself in ways that allow you to experience positive feelings of warmth, joy, and happiness?

Spiritually. Do you treat yourself to spiritually uplifting experiences such as attending church services you enjoy, reading the Bible, listening to inspirational messages, or meeting with others who share your spiritual values? Do you take time to be quiet, to pray, and to reflect on the spiritual side of life?

Financially. Do you keep yourself aware of your financial status and take routine steps to keep your finances in balance? Do you have some money designated to be used for you and your needs? Do you take steps to maintain and enjoy financial freedom from debt and chaos?

Intellectually. Are you feeding your mind on that which you find interesting and growth producing? Are you in the process of learning something new? Do you build relationships with people who stimulate your intellect and encourage intellectual development?

Socially. Do you spend time with adults whose company you enjoy? Are you able to participate in activities you find enjoyable? Do you spend time developing friendships and meeting new people? Do you spend time alone with your husband (if you're married) or developing other romantic interests (if you're not married)? Do you participate in any groups or clubs of interest to you? Do you participate in any hobbies you enjoy?

Other family relationships. Do you keep in touch with those in your extended family whose company you enjoy? Do you take time each week to keep the romance alive in your marriage? Do you set boundaries that limit the amount of unhealthy meddling allowed in your immediate family by those in your extended family?

List what you do to take care of yourself in the following ways:

- Physically
- Emotionally
- Spiritually
- Financially
- Intellectually
- Socially
- Other family relationships

Are you aware of unresolved grief, addictions, or compulsions that interfere with being a world-class mother?

ACTION

Today, write out at least three other types of goals that you will begin to process to balance your life. (Choose from creative, intellectual, educational, recreational, travel, spiritual, social, financial, etc.) Make a section for your notebook entitled "Other Goals," and put this list in your notebook to work on later.

Talk to someone about the deeper hurts that may interfere with mothering.

We're Looking for a Few Good Role Models

We all need role models and mentors to help us put into action the behavior we desire. In generations past and in other cultures, women were interwoven into an extended family that met the needs of children and helped educate girls in the fine art of mothering. With our transient culture and a majority of mothers working to provide income for the family, we have lost the tightly knit fellowship that used to allow girls an informal apprenticeship in mothering while they were growing up.

Perhaps some women place so much blame on their mothers because they assume that everything they *didn't* learn was supposed to have been taught by their mothers. Even in biblical times that was not the sole responsibility of an individual mother; it was the collective responsibility of the community of women. The Bible admonishes all women to help one another learn to become better mothers: "The older women likewise, that they be reverent in behavior, not slanderers, not given to much wine, teachers of good things—that they admonish the young women to love their husbands, to love their children, to be discreet, chaste, homemakers" (Titus 2:3–5). It is obvious from this passage that women need one another to teach the arts of mothering and making a home.

You need to put together a jigsaw puzzle of sorts to gain the whole picture of a loving woman who exhibits the qualities of a world-class mother. You may have to be creative in looking for role models and mentors. Identify the qualities that you admire in other women: acquaintances, authors, even fictional characters. As you consider their lives, you can test out and develop some of the positive qualities.

PERSONAL EVALUATION

Check off any of these areas or facets of life where you could use some help:

- Positive attitude
- Skill in disciplining children
- Beauty and grooming
- Creating a home
- Intellectual growth
- Integrity
- Showing unconditional love
- Demonstrating reliability and dependability
- Others

For each area of life you checked, list names of possible role models. Think of women you know in your family, friends, or parents of other children.

ACTION

Of the people you noted, choose three you know well enough to call on a friendly basis. Today call one of them and let her know that you're working on polishing up your mothering skills and that she is one of the people who inspires you. Let her know that you look to her as a role model. If you have the courage, you may want to ask for her encouragement and support as you continue to learn and grow as a mother.

REFLECTION

Did you readily find role models and mentors to make contact with and draw from? If someone told you that she looked up to you as a mentor in some aspect of mothering, what do you think that would be?

AFFIRMATION

As you begin to look for the good in others, you will develop those qualities as well.

Identifying Resources

Tremendous resources are available for every imaginable facet of mothering. Once you have identified specific goals and objectives, it becomes fairly easy to find resources to give you the knowledge you need, help you develop the skills you want, and provide practical assistance and support.

Listing many specific resources would not be beneficial since each person taking the journey is focused on her own goals. So, I want to give you some ideas about how to track down the resources you need. You probably have access to more resources than you could ever exhaust just working through your local library, your telephone directory, and your telephone. Here are the steps to finding resources in any area of interest.

Step One

Identify the area where you need help or more information. (You have already done this.)

Step Two

Check at your local library for books on the topic or related topics. You can go to the card catalog, a file of cards that represents every book available through the library. The cards are listed by topic and by author's last name. Most libraries have a wide variety of books on parenting and mothering. Or ask a librarian to recommend some books on the topic or guide you to the section of the library that holds the books you need.

Step Three

Contact organizations that are set up to deal with issues related to your area of interest. A great resource for family-related issues is Focus on the Family. You can call and receive leads about almost any conceivable family issue. The telephone number is 719-531-3400.

- Another way to track down groups and organizations is to use your telephone directory. Look under city, county, state, and federal governments for numbers of agencies. If you are not sure that a particular agency can help you, call and explain what information or help you are trying to locate. Staff persons will usually know where to direct you if they cannot help you.
- A growing network of treatment centers and recovery groups has resources available. You can contact counseling offices, treatment centers, or universities and usually get leads about people, groups, or organizations that help individuals in specific ways.
- You can call the offices of radio talk shows that

deal with issues related to your area of interest. Radio talk programs have to keep an extensive listing of guests who address various topics. They will probably have a list of referrals to groups and organizations as well.

• The best resources are human resources. Within your community, there are church groups, women's groups, recovery groups, parenting groups, educational seminars, and so on. To tap into these meetings, you can contact your local Chamber of Commerce.

If you are struggling with issues that are shameful, you can take refuge in the anonymity afforded by the telephone. Call a toll-free number to an appropriate hotline. Call the customer service line of a bookstore or publisher and have the books you need mailed to you directly. You can even get professional psychological counseling over the phone without ever having to leave the security of your own home.

The real key to finding information and resources is to keep on seeking, keep on asking, and keep on knocking. Once you know what you want to accomplish, what tasks you need to complete to reach your goals, what information or help you lack, it's just a matter of persistent effort to track down the resources.

PERSONAL EVALUATION

• What are three things you can do today to begin

tracking down the kind of information that you need to reach your goals?

ACTION

Do those three things!

On the back of each goal sheet in your notebook, keep track of the resources you have located that move you toward your goal.

REFLECTION

How far did you get in finding the help you need? Are you encouraged or discouraged by the process of actually reaching out toward your goals?

Establishing a Support Network

When you are involved in an ongoing process of growth, you need support and encouragement. As noted when you looked at the importance of role models and mentors, you can't develop fully all alone. Some of your long-term goals will be positively affected if a small group of people knows your aspirations and will hold you accountable to stay on track. They should be people who care for you, share your values, and are willing to press their lives into yours in an affirming way.

Some support groups are established with specific themes, such as Mothers of Pre-schoolers, Adult Children of Alcoholics, Incest Survivors, Parents Without Partners. If an issue in your life takes precedence over all others at the moment or an issue needs the sensitive compassion of others who share similar struggles, locate an appropriate group and attend the meetings. If you feel intimidated, find a good friend or relative to go with you until you feel more comfortable.

Other more general groups allow for the development of supportive relationships. These would be churchwomen's groups or Bible studies, groups working together for school- or civic-related purposes, groups for recreational activities, and so on. Within these more general groups you may be able to find one to be of genuine support to you.

Whenever you are "trying out" a support group, commit yourself to attend for at least six weeks to allow yourself and the other group members to get a sense of relationship.

If you can't find a particular group focused on an issue that you need to deal with, you can begin a support group fairly easily. Chances are that someone else out there is also hoping to find someone who understands what you are going through. If you can find one other person who shares a common need, the two of you can get the word out in the circles where you would be likely to find others to join you.

Get support that builds up your family. However, all of your support should not come from within the immediate family. You can benefit greatly from having access to the perspective of a group that can help you reflect objectively on your life. Also getting some support from outside your family may relieve the burden on your husband and children if you have been relying on them to fulfill all of your needs.

PERSONAL EVALUATION

- To whom can you turn for support as you make gains in terms of personal and spiritual growth?
- To whom have you made yourself accountable in

terms of continuing to move toward the worthwhile goals you seek?

ACTION

List the names of the people who act as a network of support for you, and describe one way each encourages your continuing pursuit of your mothering goals.

REFLECTION

How have you grown over the course of this journey to be able or willing to reach out to others and form a support network?

Sharing With or Coping Without a Partner

If you are married, you will need to parent your children together as a team. You share the overall responsibility for the rearing and discipline of your children with your spouse. You need to synchronize your efforts to be a world-class mother with the goals and life-style of your husband.

You can do two things to ease this process. First, make your goals in such a way that achieving them does not require you to control the behavior of everyone else in the home. If your goal is "to have a quiet and peaceful home where beautiful classical music can be heard wafting down the hallways every morning before breakfast," you may have a problem if your husband enjoys listening to the morning news on the radio while he dresses. Second, share your goals with your husband and also share the areas where you need extra encouragement to stay on track.

If you are not married, you will need a close-knit support group with whom to share your goals and from whom to receive help. When you look back over the areas of need you listed previously, identify persons you can turn to for help in doing the things that need to be done for your children that you can't do on your own. Clearly communicate how much you would value the support and assistance of the people who can fill some of the gaps that you cannot fill.

Personal Evaluation

If You Are Married

- Have you shared your dreams, goals, and plans with your husband? If not, what keeps you from being able to do so?
- Have you expressed what you are trying to accomplish and identified the areas in which you feel the need for extra sensitivity and support to help keep you on track?

If You Are Not Married

- Have you identified persons to help cover the needs of your children?
- Have you communicated these needs to the people involved and received commitments from them to give you and your children the necessary support?

Action

Set aside a specially designated time to discuss with your husband your 30-day journey and some of what you have been experiencing. How will any changes you will be making affect your husband's schedule and the role he will need to play in your ongoing journey?

Clearly define your expectations in terms of your husband's cooperation. If your expectations conflict with his, negotiate expectations and commitments to best meet the needs of the entire family.

If you are not married, list who acts as support persons to your family. Discuss your 30-day journey with them and plan how their involvement in your family may change as you make changes.

REFLECTION

Have you been able to clearly communicate your goals and your emotional commitment to those goals in a way that those people whose cooperation you need understand where your lives fit together?

Holding On and Letting Go

The wisdom of King Solomon was evident when he said, "To everything there is a season, a time for every purpose under heaven" (Eccles. 3:1). In parenting there are seasons as well: a time for holding on and a time for letting go. When your children are very young, they need the security of being held tightly. They are utterly dependent on you. As they grow, they become able to do for themselves the things that they once needed you to do for them. You are in a process of affirming your children's abilities so that they can learn to do the things required to become productive adults who no longer need you to take care of them. One key aspect of being a world-class mother is launching young adults who are ready to face life in the real world.

Good Housekeeping magazine (September, 1991) reports,

The primary task of families and schools is to teach children to become productive, independent adults. But it is increasingly evident that many of today's youngsters do *not* learn the basic skills they need to live and work productively. Millions of teens graduate barely knowing how to read, write, solve simple math problems, or balance a checkbook. They don't know how to write a resume or look for a job. On the domestic front, they can't cook, clean, do laundry, or sew on a button.

Somehow in the years after they are born or brought into your family, you have the responsibility to convey to your children the confidence and the skills necessary to stand on their own and become productive members of society. This is not only in the practical matters touched on by the *Good Housekeeping* article but also in the spiritual realm. God has commanded parents to pass down their knowledge of Him as well.

Listen to the command God gave the parents in the nation of Israel:

Hear, O Israel: The LORD our God, the LORD is one! You shall love the LORD your God with all your heart, with all your soul, and with all your strength. And these words which I command you today shall be in your heart. You shall teach them diligently to your children, and shall talk of them when you sit in your house, when you walk by the way, when you lie down, and when you rise up (Deut. 6:4–7).

All along you are to convey to your children your values, your faith in God, and the skills they need to succeed.

How are you supposed to do that? A little at a time. In all successful training endeavors there are four phases: (1) I do it for you; (2) I do it and you watch; (3) You do it and I watch; and (4) You do it and I do something else. For each child you can identify certain tasks at any of the given phases of training. For example:

TAYLOR (age two)
- I do it for you: Making meals.
- I do it and you watch: Putting on shoes and socks.
- You do it and I watch: Putting away small toys.
- You do it and I do something else: "Building" with blocks.

CASEY (age six)
- I do it for you: Braiding her hair.
- I do it and you watch: Using the computer.
- You do it and I watch: Reading a book.
- You do it and I do something else: Taking a bath.

The ideal is to teach them to be as self-sufficient and as confident in their own abilities as possible at each stage of development. When they are not able to meet their needs, you should make sure those needs are met. As they become more capable, you should train them to make wise decisions and develop the skills to take care of themselves.

If you continue to do for them what you should be teaching them to do for themselves, you do them a great injustice. They will not be equipped to face life.

PERSONAL EVALUATION

Consider the tasks on the following list. Use a number to designate where you think each age group should be in the launching process for that particular task.

1 = I do it for you.
2 = I do it and you watch.
3 = You do it and I watch.
4 = You do it and I do something else.

Skill	Infant	Preschool	Six to Twelve	Teen	Young Adult
Feeding	1	2–3	3–4	4	4
Dressing					
Dental hygiene					
Brushing hair					
Bathing					
Washing hair					
Choosing clothes					
Cooking					
Handling finances					
School decisions					
Choosing friends					
Choosing foods					
Use of time					
Hobbies to pursue					
Education choices					
Religious education					
Dating choices					
Determining bedtime					
Getting a job					

ACTION

Now go back to the evaluation and circle any areas where you feel that more in-depth training is needed to prepare them for life.

List what you want to convey to your children before they leave the nest. Include the following:

- Things you want them to know how to do
- Values
- Domestic skills
- Coping skills
- Knowledge
- Marriage and relationships
- Other

Dorothy Canfield Fisher said, "A mother is not a person to lean on but a person to make leaning unnecessary." In what areas have you done a good job of helping your children stand on their own two feet?

FOOD FOR THOUGHT

The mother-child relationship is paradoxical and, in a sense, tragic. It requires the most intense love on the mother's side, yet this very love must help the child grow away from the mother and to become fully independent.

—Erich Fromm

Partnering with Your Children

In setting your sights on being a world-class mother you should remain sensitive to the feedback from your children regarding their needs.

Consider the example of Marie and her children. Brenda started junior high school this year, and Stanley is in high school. Marie reads a lot of books to help her maintain a positive relationship with her kids, and she tries to apply whatever she is learning. But sometimes, "going by the book" can be annoying to the real people she is "practicing" on. Her sensitivity allows her to adjust the messages of the "experts" to fit Brenda and Stanley.

After reading books that stressed the importance of giving teens plenty of physical affection, Marie decided to begin hug therapy immediately. Her objective was specified: twelve hugs a day! Well, about the same time Marie set her objective, Stanley entered a phase where he did *not* feel comfortable being hugged by Mom. There was some good-natured bantering. Stanley would tap Marie twelve times with his finger and say, "Ah, there, Mom, I got my touches for the day. You don't have to worry about me now."

Instead of forcing the issue, Marie recognized the obstacle, stepped back, and took stock of what she was really after with the prescribed hugs. She wanted to maintain some sort of positive physical contact with her child, even if he felt he was too big to be hugged. One evening while they were watching TV, Stanley put his feet up on Marie's lap, and she began massaging his feet. He loved it and asked her to massage his feet at other times. Marie has taken the truth of the principle being taught in the books and added the element of listening to her child to determine how best to meet his needs.

God created your children and placed them in your care. Just as you were given to them to accomplish certain purposes in their character development, they have been placed by God in your life to develop your character in unique ways. Learning to love always develops character.

Although you can direct them, your children are not robots that you are "responsible" to control. One expert points out, "Child care is a two-way street, with child and care-giver influencing each other mutually and continuously, rather than a one-way street that runs only from care-giver to child." By realizing that the relationship is a two-way street, you can relax somewhat and receive from your children their perspective, their love, and their input into the relationship. You can talk with them (at the age when they can understand) about your dreams for them, about your goal to be a world-class mother, and the things you are trying to do to help them grow. If you are willing to listen to them, they can give you a clear sense of some things they need from you.

Allow them to partner with you in achieving common goals that will benefit the entire family, and allow them to learn valuable skills including domestic ones.

PERSONAL EVALUATION

- Is your relationship with your children a two-way street?
- What common goals do you share with your children?
- How do you allow your children to partner with you to keep the household running smoothly?

ACTION

If your children are old enough to understand, share with them some of what you have been learning and doing during your 30-day journey.

Ask them what they think about your evaluation of what needs to be strengthened. Stop talking and listen to what they think.

Ask them how they feel about your focusing on being a world-class mother. Stop talking and listen.

FOOD FOR THOUGHT

If a child is to keep alive his inborn sense of wonder,

he needs the companionship of at least one adult who can share it, rediscovering with him the joy, excitement, and mystery of the world we live in.

—Rachel Carson

Applying the Serenity Prayer

The Serenity Prayer says,

> God, grant me the serenity
> to accept the things I cannot change,
> courage to change the things I can,
> and the wisdom to know the difference.

You need this kind of serenity when you are raising your children. There will be things that you wish you could change but find they are out of your control. There will be areas where you will have to stand your ground, using all your courage to battle the forces that threaten your children's well-being. There will be other times when you're just not sure what to do. You need serenity from God, and you need God Himself to be there for you when you agonize over decisions.

Your heart's desire is to be a world-class mother. And in that capacity you long to spare your children the slings and arrows of this fallen world. The truth is that you cannot spare them the pain of being human and living in a world where things are not as they should be.

You can only do your best to meet their needs and

leave the rest in the hands of God. The best you can do is the best *you* are capable of doing in terms of applying yourself diligently to fulfill your role and responsibilities as a mother, to nurture a loving relationship with each child, and to bring out the best in your children, equipping them to face life as capable adults.

PERSONAL EVALUATION

- Do you do the best you can to meet your children's needs?
- When you can't meet their needs fully, do you turn their lives over to the care of God?

ACTION

Memorize the Serenity Prayer, and pray it today with reference to your children.

FOOD FOR THOUGHT

For I know the thoughts that I think toward you, says the Lord, thoughts of peace and not of evil, to give you a future and a hope.

—Jeremiah 29:11

Measuring and Rewarding Progress

The most exciting thing about taking any journey is arriving at the destination. This fact never escapes children, especially when the family is taking a long drive. "Are we there yet?" is a familiar chorus. Allow yourself some of that childlike enthusiasm about your journey. Gain the confidence to see yourself as a world-class mother. See yourself reaching your goals and arriving at your destination.

Although you may not feel like a world-class mother yet, you should be able to see that you have reached some of your specific goals. Achieving those goals represents arriving at your destination. As you continue to set and reach goals, you will feel confident that you are the best mother you can be. You will know that you are doing a good job of fulfilling your role, meeting your responsibilities, and bringing out the best in your children.

PERSONAL EVALUATION

Today you will evaluate how much you have learned and accomplished. Go back to the ratings in days 10 and 11 and revise your evaluation based on the changes you have made.

- What have you discovered about yourself?
- What steps (no matter how small) have you made in the right direction?
- What have you learned that will help you be a world-class mother?
- How has your self-image improved in terms of how you see yourself as a mother?
- Have you faithfully applied yourself to each of the thirty days on this journey?

ACTION

Write specifically what aspects of your mothering role and relationships you have strengthened and revitalized.

List the commitments you have made, the actions you have taken, and the work you have put in over the last month.

Review each goal you have recorded in your notebook, and update your status on each task that has taken you toward your goals. Identify specific goals you have achieved.

If you had a companion for the journey, take some time today to affirm and applaud each other on specific achievements.

REFLECTION

Taking a journey is a great deal more than reading a travel brochure. Consider what has taken place inside your heart, mind, emotions, and relationships as you have taken this 30-day journey. What are some of your fondest memories and discoveries from your journey?

AFFIRMATION

You have invested your time in a journey to become a world-class mother. You have taken the steps and expended the energy needed to make positive changes in your life. Your family will reap the benefits of your personal growth for years to come. Congratulations! You deserve a reward. Do something today to celebrate your progress.

FOOD FOR THOUGHT

Strength and dignity are her clothing,
    and she laughs at the time to come.
She opens her mouth with wisdom,
    and the teaching of kindness is on her tongue.
She looks well to the ways of her household,
    and does not eat the bread of idleness.
Her children rise up and call her blessed.
                —Prov. 31:25–28 NRSV

The Continuing Journey

You have come to the end of the 30-day journey outlined in this book, and you have probably come to recognize that you are the mother your children need, even though you may have identified some areas that need continued attention.

Being a world-class mother has been defined to mean balancing your resources and abilities in each of three areas: fulfilling your role and responsibilities, developing loving relationships, and seeing the good in your children and bringing out the best in them. As you continue to keep this kind of healthy balance, you really are a world-class mother.

You have taken decisive action to learn new things about each area. You have a notebook with goal sheets and forms to follow toward achieving your worthy goals. Why stop now? Each time you achieve one of your goals in each area, choose another to replace it. In this way you will continue to grow and find a sense of confidence that comes from knowing you are moving in the right direction.

The important thing is not to lose momentum. Each day, one day at a time, keep your dreams clearly in sight, your goals well defined, your tasks identified, your obstacles targeted for attack, and your relationships growing. The journey continues.

PERSONAL EVALUATION

As we part ways at the end of this journey I would like to share an observation from my own life about making personal evaluations. On a recent evening I was on my own, caring for my three children (ages seven, two, and one), along with another seven-year-old girl. I was a bit on edge, tired, and hungry. Since there were four of them and one of me, I knew I would have to be creative if we were to have a nice evening together. I decided to take them to the restaurant my husband manages before venturing out to see Christmas lights. In the waiting area I received numerous wary smiles and various comments about how brave I was to attempt dinner alone with this energetic bunch of kids. I managed to get through dinner without any major catastrophes, although my personal evaluation of how I was doing was clouded as I caught flying bits of bananas midair, commended excellence in menu coloring, rescued tumbling tumblers of milk, and managed to consume a few chicken fingers and an occasional french fry. When I finally strapped the children into the van seats, I was relieved to have made it through the meal.

My husband arrived home some hours later with this report. A couple at a nearby table worked for child protective services. They had been watching me deal with the kids and were evaluating my performance. They called my husband over and asked him to tell me that they were very impressed with how well I cared for the children in what was obviously a challenging situation.

I was genuinely surprised. If I had been asked to evaluate myself, I would not have given the same report. I would never have recognized how well I had done. I was too busy averting potential disaster. You too probably miss seeing how very well you care for your children. The fact that you have taken a journey such as this commends you highly. As you grow in your mothering, I encourage you to give yourself the pat on the back that you deserve far more than you probably realize.

ACTION

Decide whether you want to work through this 30-day journey a second time, now that you are familiar with the process.

Decide whether you want to continue using your personal growth notebook to record and monitor your progress.

Forgive yourself for any shortcomings in the past and make a commitment to move forward and make positive choices to overcome obstacles that may present themselves in the future.

REFLECTION

After taking your journey, do you have a sense of balance in all three areas? Are you taking clearly defined steps and making commitments to achieve balance in all three areas? Are you ready to see yourself as a world-class mother?

FOOD FOR THOUGHT

We cannot do everything at once, but we can do something at once.

—Calvin Coolidge

Suggested Reading

Arterburn, Stephen, and Dave Stoop. *When Someone You Love Is Someone You Hate.*

Bradshaw, John. *Bradshaw on the Family.*

——. *Healing the Shame That Binds You.*

Buehler, Rich. *Love: No Strings Attached.*

Campbell, Ross. *How to Really Love Your Child.*

——. *How to Really Love Your Teenager.*

Hull, Karen. *The Mommy Book.*

Murray, Marilyn. *Prisoner of Another War.*

Ortlund, Anne. *Disciplines of the Beautiful Woman.*

Schofield, Deniece. *Confessions of a Happily Organized Family.*

Swindoll, Charles. *You and Your Child.*

Sometimes problems are too difficult to handle alone on a 30-day journey. If you feel that you need additional help, please talk with one of the counselors at New Life Treatment Centers. The call is confidential and free.

1-800-277-LIFE